D0327640

Mom As You Are

Daily wisdom for
Moms who lose
it and want to
mindfully get it back

Mom As You Are

Daily wisdom for
Moms who lose
it and want to
mindfully get it back

DAWN OBEIDALLAH DAVIS PhD, ERYT 500

Mom As You Are

Daily wisdom for Moms who lose it and mindfully want to get it back

Prentice Press Publishing House
12 Prentice Rd
Newton, MA 02459

© 2019 by Dawn Obeidallah Davis

All rights reserved. No part of this book may be reproduced in any form or by any means, electronic or mechanical, including photocopying, recording, or by any information storage and retrieval system, without permission in writing from the author.

Cover and text design: meadencreative.com

Davis, Dawn

Mom As You Are: Daily Wisdom For Moms Who Lose It and Want To Mindfully Get It Back.—1st ed.

ISBN: 978-0-9600545-0-3 (paperback)

Dedication

Dedicated to my three little loves —Julia, Grace and Charlotte, who teach me daily what it means to Mom As You Are.

There is no single effort more radical in its potential for saving the world than a transformation of the way we raise our children.

Marianne Williamson

Walk openly and flawed right into the present moment armed with wisdom, a willingness to learn and a good sense of humor.

Dawn Davis, April 2018

PREFACE

Mom as you are, exactly as you are, right in this moment.

Raising a family rocks—and at times—rocks your world in some not-so-great ways. I don't know about you, but I haven't experienced anything quite as meaningful and poignant, nor as exhausting, anxiety-provoking, and frustrating as raising my children. We have all had those days when we feel like a rockstar about our choices, our kids, our lives—followed by days where the poop repeatedly hits the fan. The truth is that we all lose it sometimes. It happens, it's natural, and no matter how pressed and polished the neighbor appears, it's happening in her home, too. Not a one of us is free from these bumps and bruises along the journey. Embracing this reality is the groundwork for some really deep growth and healing.

This book is an invitation to loosen the grip on yourself. Parenting is hard, and we can either be our own best ally or tear ourselves down. Recognize that you are a great mom, doing your level best, moment after moment, raising your amazing children. Acknowledge the fact that sometimes you feel like crap and want to throw in the towel, and that you are also blessed to get to do this. This book is written from the trenches of motherhood and knows that even though our culture might have sold us an impossible dream of perfection, that we show up every day, strong and resilient and we rise, no matter what. This book provides both theoretical and practical applications of how to be attentive towards yourself and honor your needs with greater compassion. It offers suggestions for helping you take care of the typical suffering that we all feel. In addition, this book includes strategies for increasing your own awareness of your thoughts—which, if you are anything like me, are not always supportive! By becoming more self-aware, we offer ourselves more self-acceptance, which translates into being calmer, happier, and more emotionally-available moms.

I know how precious our time is and so I wrote this book in small chunks that can be digested and assimilated in a few minutes. Each "mom-sized bite" offers reflections on parenting challenges or experiences, with step-by-step suggestions for managing the intensity. All passages include a healing yoga pose (some are more meditations than asana), with instructions, pictures, and information about the benefits of that particular pose. You can follow us on FB: Dawn Davis Yoga and Mom As

You Are pages, as well as explore free yoga videos at www.dawndavis.com. In addition, at the end of each passage are mantras, called "Be-Kind-To-Your-Mindspeak"—daily incantations to help you relax into the present moment. You can say these out loud to yourself as you practice yoga, or even as you look into your own eyes in the mirror—which somehow is super powerful. Each entry stands on its own, so you can reach for what you need, when you need it (or read the whole thing sequentially, if you prefer).

In writing this book, I applied my skills as a Developmental Psychologist, my training and experience as a yoga teacher, insights gleaned from my own parents and teachers, and my current experiences of mothering my three lively children. I threw myself into the study of the wisdom traditions, spirituality, and scientific research on both happiness and parenting. I talked with fellow moms, my husband, my therapist. And I wrote. And wrote. Writing gave me reprieve from the constriction and sadness that occasionally marked my mothering journey. But real freedom came after sharing these writings with other moms. Think of this as a companion filled with practical suggestions for how to make peace with yourself as you work on keeping peace in your homes.

CONTENTS

INTRODUCTION

Loosen the Grip on the Mat: Why Yoga Helps You Navigate Motherhood.

Through the blur, I wondered if I was alone or if other parents felt the same way I did—that everything involving our children was painful in some way. The emotions, whether they were joy, sorrow, love or pride, were so deep and sharp that in the end they left you raw, exposed and yes, in pain. The human heart was not designed to beat outside the human body and yet, each child represented just that—a parent's heart bared, beating forever outside its chest.

Debra Ginsberg

As parents, some days we feel like heroes and other days the struggle is fierce and we falter. Regardless of the emotional climate of any day, yoga helps. For me, practicing yoga strengthens my body, improves my balance, refines my breath, and calms my mind. But, does it do anything else, specifically in regard to helping us become the most centered parents we can be? The beauty of yoga is that it offers us metaphorical and actual benefits that help navigate the choppy seas of parenting and even help us enjoy the smoother sailing times.

Patience: With the relentless tenacity of an octopus, my 10-year old begs to turn on the television, buy whatever is trending on Amazon, and stay up late—basically a daily occurrence. I'm tired of hearing myself say no, no, no. I can feel the pressure building, my own frustration mounting. I'm just about to lose it. So, I detour. I call upon the determination that we've been cultivating in those poses that we hold long, long, longer than we want to. We are not strangers to the feeling of impatience. We remember that by breathing deeply and coaching ourselves to relax into the discomfort, we discover that buried underneath the swirling chaos is something deeper. Something like a well of patience and calm determination. It's really in those ordinary situations that we want to get out of that we can access the gift to build this internal muscle. When we feel like every last button is being pushed, think of times like these as opportunities to remember how you found the calm in the storm of that long Warrior II hold—we did it one deep breath followed by another and another.

Stay Present: I'm on my 10th round of Headbanz. The monotony is such that I find myself spacing out, thinking about what I'm going to cook for dinner, the carpool arrangements, and that email I keep forgetting to send. I catch myself and bring my mind back to the present moment. This game, these children, this moment. A few seconds later, my mind wanders another path strewn with distractions. Our thoughts, especially in the quieter moments, can take flight. Just like on the mat, where our mind wanders, bringing ourselves back to the present takes conscious effort. By deeply attending to what is here and now, we wisely acknowledge that this life, all its magical and all its mundane and even boring aspects, is completely impermanent *and* totally ours to live. I remind myself of the uncomfortable truth that everything passes. And, because everything passes, wouldn't it make sense to be fully engaged in what you're doing now?

Forgive Ourselves: Sometimes we can't yoga our way out of it. And we lose our composure. Despite my best efforts, sometimes I yell at the kids or state a consequence that I have no intention of following through on. Then when I'm calmer I have to back track and undo it by giving them (and myself) another chance. And in times like these, the most important thing to remember is that even when we fall out of a yoga pose, yoga asks us to get back up on our feet. To forgive ourselves for not being perfect. In fact, to embrace the truth that we are not perfect with a little umph! is to embrace the fact that you are human after all. Why not give yourself the bandwidth to make mistakes, find yourself in the learning process, and therefore invite in more grace. This increases your feeling of buoyancy, of joyfulness. And your kids get to see you making mistakes, getting back up on your feet, forgiving yourself, forgiving them, and moving forward. How awesome is that?!

So, go ahead and take what you're cultivating on the mat and bring it to bear where it really counts—in your own home. Transferring those amazing skills to your parenting can be a game changer. To be more patient doesn't require anyone in our lives do anything different—as we learn in the yoga room, the real path to patience comes when we are patient with ourselves.

Wouldn't it be something if we dropped our expectations of how things "should" be and instead landed firmly into what is here and now in front of us. To be more loving to all concerned, can you honor yourself with compassion, and possibly trust in your own resilience, as well as deepen your respect for your process? As you already know—the practice is ongoing, and that's why returning to it time and again bolsters our inner fortitude and capacity to be present with ourselves as we are present with our families.

Let me say at the outset that this is NOT a book on how to raise perfect kids or how to be a perfect mom. In fact, your kids don't need a perfect mom. They need the mom that you already are to show up with self-acceptance, acknowledgment of your amazing strengths and very human flaws. I wish you well on your journey, fellow traveler.

GET CENTERED

Have you ever unwittingly thrown yourself off center because of your reaction to something your kids said or did? Yeah, well, me too. This section is all about fortifying your center so that when it hits the fan the next time, you're more likely to stay centered. It's also for those inevitable times when things roll downhill —these mindful moments will help you find ground and get centered again.

GET CENTERED:
Screw Mary Poppins

Wholehearted living…means cultivating the courage, compassion, and connection to wake up in the morning and think, no matter what gets done and how much is left undone, I am enough. It's going to bed at night thinking, Yes, I am imperfect and vulnerable and sometimes afraid, but that doesn't change the truth that I am also brave and worthy of love and belonging

Brene' Brown

I recently watched a documentary about Julie Andrews. With a wistful look in his eye, the interviewer asked Ms. Andrews whether she parented her real-life children the way Mary Poppins and Maria Von Trapp in The Sound of Music did. She graciously shook her head, "Well, those mothers are perfect. They have to be. It's always perfect on screen." Phew.

Despite what Hollywood is peddling, perfect parenting is a crock. Glossy all the time—that belongs on the cutting room floor of a photo shopper's apartment. Never upset, always having the right answer, the right "look", the perfect kids, the perfect everything—is a one-way ticket to crazytown.

Maybe you can relate to this before-school-triathalon: one kid was sick and lying on the couch; the other two were in each other's hair screaming. My husband was already at work, the carpool was idling in the driveway, and the eggs were burned. I didn't sleep well the night before, so I had even less in emotional reserves. The frustration welled up inside me and before I could even stop myself, I was yelling like I was a contestant on *Survivor*. My day was off to a pretty rocky start.

It's true that if I had been more centered, the irritations wouldn't have gotten to me quite so deeply. But, that's water under the bridge, because I wasn't in a more centered state before it hit the fan. And I certainly wasn't in a more centered state after it did.

So, what to do now? How to get the train back on the tracks? The first thing is to remember that you're not alone. I swear this type of thing happens in half of the homes in the neighborhood, so please don't think you're some loser mom out there who is the only one confronting the difficult morning and those crazy feelings. Second, do NOT beat yourself up for going off the rails. It's tempting to get into harshing on ourselves, but I promise you—it will only make you feel worse, and perhaps more importantly, the guilt that follows will make you MORE likely to fall off the rails again.

Truth is, you are doing your level best, we all make mistakes, and actually, it's in the screwing up every now and again that lays the fertile soil for growth and learning. Not just for us as moms, but for our children. In fact, pediatrician and psychoanalyst Donald Winnicott argued that children don't need perfect mothering, they need "good enough mothering." In his view, the disappointments our children feel based on our not being perfect parents are actually good for their development. The logic is that the world will regularly disappoint them, the world is not perfect, and to strive for perfection in our mothering only sets them up to fail when they exit the comforts of home and enter the real world. So, rather than holding yourself hostage to some unattainable standard, congratulate yourself that you are on this path of greater awareness and change. By giving yourself space to breathe (literally), you'll also be in a better position to notice what may have been the background context that made the conditions ripe to destabilize your peace of mind. For instance, being overstressed, or overcommitted, or not getting enough sleep, or feeling depleted may be just a few ingredients that contribute to throwing you off your center. Noting whatever is going on in the background is essential because it can help you, within reason, to prioritize whatever you need to support yourself, so you can create more internal grounding and space.

Once you have the background context identified, then it's time to dig deeper. Was there a "trigger"? For some of us, this is garden-variety stuff—for others, like myself—it can include traumatic memories of something in my childhood. Then, I'm in a nearly traumatized state myself, fighting against something that happened decades ago, but that some protective aspect of my mind believes is in the present moment. In any case, full and deep breaths are a quick way to bring yourself back to a calmer center. What might it take for you to be even a little more patient and kind towards yourself when you make the inevitable mistakes?

Deeper respect for yourself also might include touching base with your spouse, or a trusted friend or relative to debrief about the situation. You don't have to "vent" per se, but letting another know what you've been through can be very healing. Alternatively, journaling about your experience and identifying reasonable plans to nurture yourself can offer great relief, too. These efforts will help you relax and renew as you embark on the next moment.

Together, we have an opportunity to dethrone Mary Poppin's "practically perfect in every way" and the haunting guilt that shows up when we feel we've fallen short. This time in your life is incredibly precious. Don't throw it away trying to be some perfect version of you. We each deserve more acceptance of and respect for ourselves as we make our way up and down this mountain. Breathing deeply can calm your nervous system and help you pause to find center. You are now positioned to enjoy this phase of life with honesty, creativity and an aliveness that never occurred to Ms. Poppins.

HEALING YOGA POSE: *Malasana.* (Garland Pose). Stand with your feet slightly turned out so the toes point outward and heels are slightly turned in. The distance between your feet should be broader than hip-width distance. With your core engaged, hinge back with your hips and come into a squatted position, allowing your hips to drop towards the ground. Keep your core engaged. If your heels pick up off the floor, place blocks under your them so that your lower body is supported. At this point, you can press your hands together, with elbows nudging your thighs open, or for a more advanced option, reach your arms behind your legs and take hold of the backs of your ankles. Breathe here for 5-10 slow and deep breaths. Maintain core engagement as you come to a standing forward fold.

BENEFITS: *Releases tension in the hips through opening the inner thighs* *and groins. Strengthens your ankles and feet. Breaks up tension in the upper back. Deeply relaxing.*

BE-KIND-TO-YOUR-MINDSPEAK: Today, I give myself the space to be human, to forgive myself, and to heal. The kinder I am towards myself, the more kindness I share with those around me.

Figure 1: *Malasana* (Garland Pose)

GET CENTERED:
Find Sanity

You have the power over your mind, not outside events. Realizing this, you will find strength.

Marcus Aurelius

Ever have one of those days (or ten), where you felt somehow so agitated that you couldn't be fully present with your children? I have been there, too. After many encounters with the little loves where I wasn't in my centered space, I knew I need to create a system that I could turn to when the waves of childhood threatened to capsize my internal boat. To that end, I've developed a three-part system that helps me get my attitude into a more optimal-state (most of the time).

The first step is to know whether, during a tense situation with the kids, do you feel lonely or do you feel supported? Nine times out of 10, many of us feel alone, as if we are the only one deeply concerned with what is going on. Truth is, we may be the only one on the front lines in that moment. If that is true for you, acknowledge that you feel this aloneness and —this is important—remind yourself not to get sucked into its black hole of anxiety. You are in a long ancestral line of mothers, as well as in the energetic company of moms who are actively mothering world-wide right in this very moment. Keeping it real, we are more alone now than ever before in the history of parenting—less than 100 years ago, most moms mothered their children alongside extended family members—which means that, at least on a DNA-evolutionary level, we are on fairly new territory. The informal yet structured system of other adults routinely helping is not present as it once was for our grandmothers. So, turning to other non-judgmental moms might be just what the doctor ordered. It'll help replace that feeling of loneliness with a sense of camaraderie in short order.

That being said, you never are truly alone. Sometimes I say to myself (silently!) "I am here by your side forever. I will never leave you." This somewhat corny statement helps soothe the sense of being abandoned or left with a burden too large to bear. Repeating this to myself several times in a row helps reduce any anxiety of being alone with the challenge and improves my peace of mind in even tricky moments.

The next step is much harder. It includes asking yourself, "how does my child see this situation"? For me, it's usually not the way I, her middle-aged mother, sees it. It's probably not even the way her sisters see it. Likely, it's most attuned with how her friends see it, but even that is a clumsy approximation of her individual perspective. So instead of telling her all my rules and opinions in that moment, (which I can do at any point in the future), I try to keep my mind and heart open and become genuinely receptive to her point of view. I listen as attentively as I know how. This also can be hard as hell, especially if you want the outcome to go a certain way. Remember, you can always lay down the gauntlet, but for now, just focus on what she is feeling and do everything in your power to understand how she sees the situation. Remember you can't teach someone to swim when they're already drowing; better to wait till they're calmly on the shoreline. By doing this, you'll increase your child's sense of herself, which becomes her solid foundation for healthy relationships. It shows her that love includes seeing the world through the other person's eyes—the basis of empathy—something in short supply these days.

Third, and this is the hardest one yet: find what you're grateful for in the moment. After a particularly difficult situation with one of my children, I was beside myself. I felt hopeless and really sad. Through tears, I asked myself how could I grow stronger in the process of this challenging moment? The answer was—find what I was grateful for in that awfulness. Strange, because I felt anything but gratitude in that moment. However, with not much to lose, I began to explore what I might be grateful for in that difficult moment. This shift in consciousness (rather than what the hell is wrong me with/her/situation/etc.) was followed by a great relief. I realized that this hard and unwanted situation was a great opportunity to work on my spiritual fortitude—to get me stronger by forcing me to breathe deeply to stay in the present moment. With eyes looking for gratitude, I noticed that this ugly moment actually helped me expand my point of view. I also was grateful that I had a dear childhood friend that I could reach out to to get her thoughts on the situation (first tool), which helped me stay centered and then allowed me to see the situation from another point of view, including the perspective of my daughter (second tool). I felt grateful for the chance to help work with my daughter and to realign her attitude as well as my own. The edge of frustration dissolved a little bit.

Look for ways to use your resources, including your connection to yourself. Deepen your understanding of their perspective and compassion for what you both are going through. Finally, notice what gifts the difficult situation is offering. It won't take away your frustrations entirely, but it will allow you to hold within you that still small space where you can better access your peace of mind. Working with these tools can help us transform the parenting challenges into ones that feel calmer and ultimately, more satisfying.

HEALING YOGA POSE: *Supta Baddha Konasana.* (Supine Cobbler Pose). Have two pillows or yoga blocks nearby and lie on your back. Bend your knees and place your feet on the floor. Now join the soles of your feet together so that your knees open out to the sides. Leave space between your groins and your heels so that you are not overstraining. If this feels like too much pressure on the inner groins, place yoga blocks or blankets underneath each leg at the mid-thigh point for support. Placing one hand on your heart and one on your abdomen. Do you notice how your hands rise on the inhale and fall on the exhale? Breathe deeply and slowly for 20-50 luxurious breaths.

BENEFITS: *Gently stretches the groins and inner thighs. Allows spine to relax and encourages the muscles of the upper back to let go. Improves overall circulation. Helps relieve cramps and bloating, can elevate mood.*

BE-KIND-TO-YOUR-MINDSPEAK: I am centered and calm. I feel the earth supporting me under my feet. Today I access my strength through my peacefulness.

Figure 2: *Supta Baddha Konasana* (Supine Cobbler Pose)

GET CENTERED: FIND SANITY

GET CENTERED:
Disorganized Crime in the Kitchen Drawers

A pessimist sees the difficulty in every opportunity; an optimist sees the opportunity in every difficulty.

Winston Churchill

Seeing a bank of well-ordered kitchen drawers somehow makes me feel that the world is in order. BUT, I'm not a natural organizer when it comes to "stuff". So, it was with some degree of existential agony that I opened several drawers I had spent hours organizing, only to find them rummaged through (by someone who shall remain nameless) and left in utter disarray.

In the grand scheme of things, no big deal. But on the visceral level of wanting order out of the chaos of my days, big deal. Grateful that all of the usual suspects still were asleep when I entered the kitchen, I could take a few moments to recalibrate my reaction and get perspective. I could have dismissed my own feelings, or in an opposite fashion, I could have flipped out. But I've learned (the hard way) that pretending away my daily frustration, or indulging it by acting out, only serves to lay planks of resentment and a future explosion.

I let my feelings of annoyance and anger come up, without pushing them down and without blowing them out of proportion. Feeling emotions, not feeding the emotions is a skill, just like any other skill. It requires that we get quiet and allow whatever is there to bubble up, committing not to act it out. Cause you know, my typical response might have been to yell at the suspected messer-upper, and maybe even take away a privilege. I reasoned to myself that yelling at the responsible party would help my sticky feelings dissipate in short order. Yet, I knew that the uncomfortable feelings would quickly be replaced by guilt—not great. And, since I've lost faith in the idea that yelling teaches kids anything anyway, I opted for plan B.

Plan B. I waited for the likely offender to wake up. During that time, I practiced yoga for about 15 minutes, and got physically centered. Practicing also offered an embodied reminder that even in poses, difficult feelings come up and the best way to deal with those feelings is to stick with the pose breath by breath. Residing right under that layer of stress, our composure is present.

After the likely suspect settled into the morning, I brought her back to the kitchen to help me face the messed-up drawers. I told her that I'd help her, and together we could put everything back in order. To my surprise, she did it all herself.

I can't say it always works out so smoothly. Sometimes it's hard enough to hold it together, but on those occasions when we can use annoying situations as opportunities to center ourselves, things shift. With mindful determination, we can use the appearance of unwanted events as a signal to deeply relax. It is a sign to feel the emotion, as unpleasant as it may be, and to commit to connecting with breath. This allows us to let go, find our center, and reveals something even more profound about accessing a calmer space, even when events may be challenging superficially.

Let today be the day that you embrace and relax around the moments that threaten your peace of mind. Rather than rail against them, see them as your golden opportunity to sharpen your capacity to center yourself. The more you approach the little frustrations in this way, the better your ability to stay grounded during the even bigger swells of life.

HEALING YOGA POSE: *Parsvotonasana.* (Pyramid Pose). Place your right foot toward the top of your mat, toes pointing forward. Your left heel is about three feet behind your right heel. Turn your left toes to a 45-degree angle, toes pointing to the left side of the mat. If this feels too restrictive in your hips, then move your left foot to the left a little more so you attain a hip-width distance stance. Inhale both arms up to the ceiling, palms facing each other. Both hip bones are facing forward and both legs are straight. Place your right hand at the crease between your right thigh and your right hip. As you exhale, reach your torso forward and extend your left arm longer toward the front of the room. Breathe one full breath with your chest parallel to the floor. Peel your right hip back with your right hand, then let both hands drop down towards the floor or blocks. On your next exhale, drop your torso closer towards your right leg. You'll feel a stretch through the back of the right leg into the hamstrings. Breathe for

8-12 breaths. Come up to standing on an inhale, with slightly bent knee and a straight spine. Repeat on the other side.

BENEFITS: *Stretches the entire length of the back body, especially the hamstrings. Relieves congestion in the spinal nerves, all while increasing your vitality. Enhances serenity and connection to the present moment.*

BE-KIND-TO-YOUR-MINDSPEAK: I will look at today's challenges as a signal to relax and access my deeper wisdom. I use my breath to bring my mind home to my relaxed body. Each moment is an opportunity to let go.

Figure 3: *Parsvotonasana* (Pyramid Pose)

GET CENTERED:
Your Personal Spiritual Trainer, At Your Service

Life's ups and downs provide windows of opportunities to determine your values and goals. Think of using all obstacles as stepping stones to build the life you want.

Marsha Sinetar

In the late 1970's, my Dad attempted to irrigate our family's property. He was armed with a couple of shovels and a few picks, along with an impressive determination. His intention was to remove the dirt and rocks that blocked the path to fresh water buried underneath the soil. As exhaustion began to seep into his bones and thoughts of giving up took hold, he turned a corner. A loud "YES!" rang through the summer heat. He couldn't have been more jubilant that afternoon had he struck gold. Dad didn't create that water. All he did was clear away the dirt and debris to reveal what was there all along. It required steadfast and persistent action, coupled with a healthy dose of faith, to gain access to that resource which then benefited the whole family.

Our efforts to be mindful mothers, to be centered as we parent, can feel buried under a pile of rubble, too. Mindful mothering can be even more elusive if we believe we are responsible for *creating* mindfulness. Similar to Dad, we are simply clearing away that which blocks us from reaching it. What covers mindfulness up? Stress, worry, distraction— to name a few. After all, we live in a culture that feeds on fear, tells us that we are doing this parenting-thing "wrong," gins up our worries that our children will be all but ruined by (the latest fill in the blank). That is why systematically cultivating internal tools to remove the gunk that gets in the way, well, it's essential.

Unlike Dad's adventure, our tools to excavate our way towards a centered mind are more internal. The good news is that our internal tools are with us all the time, never rust, and actually get sharper the more we use them. The two major tools are our breath and intention. In the shed of our hearts, these tools can be unlocked through using the Grounded Hand Posture when you just wake up in the morning. The Grounded Hand Posture is where you place one hand on your heart and one on your abdomen, and then close your eyes and inhale deeply. Pause at the top of the inhale. Exhale slowly. Pause at the bottom of the exhale. Repeat four or five times, feeling the warmth of your hands and the way your breath moves your body in a natural rhythm. Perhaps you feel a little more space. From this cleared-the-deck position, set an intention for the next hour—for instance, peace of mind, clarity, or energy. This can help when things are going well and can even help when you've got a harder climb ahead.

The practice is to pull yourself back to this intention when things are relatively calm so that when things ratchet up a few notches, it'll be easier for your mind to find this well-worn pathway. Notice I said, "*when*" things ratchet up, not "*if*". Thing is, life with kids is punctuated by moments of things ratcheting up a notch or two (or three).

Drawing on Dad's case, the largest rocks, the ones that might dash the hopes of someone with less persistence, were exactly the ones that melted his annoyance, focusing and transforming his frustration into a calmer determination. Those daunting rocks became the stepping-stones to explore his own inner well of purpose and even-keeled resolve. The rocks in our lives can be used similarly, to help us get even more resolved to stay steady and clear.

Think of the challenges the way you would a personal trainer hired to increase physical strength. The "rocks" can be looked at as spontaneous appointments with the inner spiritual trainer—helping us hone and chisel our emotional fitness. When the parenting challenges appear, instead of "oh crap, I can't believe this happened", what would it be like if you acknowledged that you don't like the situation, but then ask yourself, "How can I use this barrier to become more clear and mindful so I can be of greatest use?" or even, "How can I embrace this situation to ultimately move my family towards something even greater than initially envisioned?" Sometimes when things are particularly tough, you can remind yourself that your resolve is best developed during the heavy-lifting phase. It will get you in touch with your own personal grit and grace.

The well-water of mindful mothering has been here all along. With these internal tools, and a framework that embraces the challenges as opportunities to get more focused, we are in good shape.

HEALING YOGA POSE: *Parvitta Anjaliasana.* (Twisting Crescent Lunge Pose). Step your right foot toward the top of your mat. Your left leg is extended behind you, with toes pressing into the mat, heel lifted high. Feet are about four feet apart from each other (longways), and at least hip-width distance apart (sideways). Join your hands at your heart center in prayer position. Drop your tailbone down so that you lengthen your lower back. Take a big breath in, and on the exhale, twist to your right. Your elbow reaches past your right thigh. To lighten the load, drop your left knee to the mat. To deepen the pose, open your arms so your left hand reaches down to the floor or block (either on the inside or outside of your right foot) and your right arm reaches above you. Shoulders are stacked here. Breathe for 10 slow breaths and then release. Switch legs and repeat.

BENEFITS: *Releases tension in the side body and back body. Relaxes the hip flexor. As is the case with most twists, this pose provides an internal massage of your abdominal organs, increasing their efficiency. Develops strength in your thighs, torso, and improves your capacity to concentrate.*

BE-KIND-TO-YOUR-MINDSPEAK: I embrace each difficult moment as an opportunity to grow more centered and calm. Breath by breath, moment by moment, my spiritual staff gets stronger and my vision more clear.

Figure 4: *Parvitta Anjaliasana* (Twisting Crescent Lunge Pose)

GET CENTERED:
Fix It On The Inside—
4 Steps to Find Calm

I have so much chaos in my life, it's become normal. You become used to it. You have to just relax, calm down, take a deep breath and try to see how you can make things work rather than complain about how they're wrong.

Tom Welling

It was one of those mornings. It started over who got to the wear the white jean jacket to school. Then one of my children decided that it was a spectacular idea to toss all the books from her bookshelf onto her bedroom floor instead of eating breakfast. The lunches were half-made, the house a wreck. And the clock was ticking. Maybe you can relate to feeling like you've had a full day before 8AM.

Sometimes when the morning unfolds like this, I'm ready to boil over, yell my head off, and threaten to take away a bunch of stuff. And, if you've ever taken that path, you know it might work in the short run. In the long run, not so much. In the wake of our own temper-tantrum, we can wind up feeling guilty for modeling the exact same behavior we're wishing to extinguish. On this particular moment, the pain of anticipating feeling guilty gave me pause. Let's face it: if freaking out on them produced lasting results, we'd have figured out this whole thing long ago, right?!

Ready? You don't have to fix it. You don't have to solve the clothing war, the books will get picked up (eventually), and the children will get to school (eventually). Let go of the goal of "fixing" the external chaos and instead cultivate the goal of maintaining your peace. As Michael Singer reminds us "you don't want your happiness to be conditional upon the behavior of other people." Thing is, they might arrive a minute after the bell rings, but if we're a screaming mess, the damage of that experience far outweighs the damage of being tardy.

What to do when it's hitting the fan? Here are four suggestions to lean on when the dynamic in your house is worthy of its own YouTube Channel.

1. **Take a deep breath in and a long slow breath out**. Emphasize the exhale to reduce feeling stressed and anxious. Intentionally breathe several breaths, feeling the energy of the breath lifting you on inhale and releasing you on exhale. You can even soften the soles of your feet into the floor if you'd like additional grounding.

2. **Become consciously aware** of your internal state (anger, disappointment, etc). Awareness is Gold. Use the Buddhist or Shamanic tradition of naming the emotion to create more emotional space. It gives us distance between the situation and our thoughts. By the way, this doesn't mean gritting teeth and muttering under your breath, "I'm pissed!" It means witnessing the emotions in a more neutral way (not easy). And then, most importantly, it means noticing if the emotions brought some thoughts along with it. Thoughts like, oh I don't know, let's just call it negative self-put-downs and insults, like "I can't believe I'm in this again with them, when will they/I/the family learn?" Or "I suck", or even more subtle like, "I can't get this parenting thing right and everyone knows it." The pause of noticing the emotions and companion thoughts is paramount because it gives us space. We don't have to get pulled into the emotional maelstrom. Every feeling comes and goes, so why bother getting all bunched up in it? Instead, witnessing the feelings and steering clear of negative self-chatter will make it far less likely that we will overreact. And when we do overreact, we just might find that it's much easier to draw ourselves back to our center.

3. **Notice where in your body you feel the tension**. Most of the time, we accumulate tension in our bodies without even realizing where. Maybe your teeth are clenched, or your shoulders have collapsed forward. One of my favorite places to hold tension is in my neck and shoulders. After noticing where the tension lives, breathe into that area. A visualization I've had success using is to imagine using my inhale to pull in white light into my body. Then as I exhale, I imagine the white light escorting the stress out of my body. The tension can leave through the mouth, soles of feet, or every cell in your body. In this way, the exhale acts like a one-way portal of stress release.

4. **Commit to your own peace of mind**. So, I recently did all three of these above and guess what? I calmed down. I reminded myself that staying calm is a choice—one which beats the alternative of running

around my house like a crazy woman. And when I did all three of these things and calmed down, the kids also began to settle down. Amazing!

It lasted for precisely one and a half minutes.

If children are our greatest teachers, this was one demanding lesson plan. It was when they went back at it that I had to pull up my spiritual sleeves. This is where many of us, myself included, can throw in the towel. We initially make an effort, but if it doesn't succeed in a sustained way, we toss up our hands in resignation "see, doesn't work!" But, it does work. It just takes recommitting again and again to our peace of mind.

Remember your happiness and peace of mind is not contingent on their behavior. You can stay open and loving while you actively work the situation. As with any commitment, expect to be challenged, but remind yourself that each time you stick with it, you are increasing your capacity to handle this with greater ease.

Keeping it real—you won't see me in a Stepford-wife apron anytime soon. My house is nearly always in flux with dishevelment and I can't deny that we run late on some days. But by focusing our minds on our internal state, by consciously releasing the tension in our bodies, we can relate to our daily struggles differently. We stand the chance to free ourselves from the drama and craziness that can swirl in our lives because instead of trying to fix it on the outside, we are committed to focusing on centering our own mind and body.

This type of approach encourages us to look at these challenges as opportunities to practice holding our center. It may feel awkward at first, but the more we embrace the chaos as if it were a chance to practice calming our internal reactions, the more we free our energy to deal with our life in a more balanced way.

HEALING YOGA POSE: *Uttitha Hastasana* (Standing Mountain Pose with Arms Above). Stand with your big toe joints together (or feet hip-width distance, if more comfortable). Now bring your mind to the four corners of each foot: the big toe mound, the pinky toe mound, and the inner and outer heels. Press down evenly through all four corners of each foot. Next, align the crown of your head with your perineum, so your spine stands tall in one elegant line. Release any gripping in your butt muscles. Spiral your inner thighs towards each other and behind you. On an inhale, raise your arms overhead. Let your fingertips reach towards the ceiling as you release and soften any tension along the tops of your shoulders. Take 5-10 breaths here.

BENEFITS: *Grounding pose. Elevates mood. Encourages good posture. Each breath is intended to release and relax your body and mind. Your mind may wander, that's part of the process. The most important thing is that you gently bring your mind back to the conscious experience of your breath. Stretches the tops of the shoulders and the sides of the torso.*

BE-KIND-TO-YOUR-MINDSPEAK: My breath is my anchor to clarity and compassion for myself and others. I am committed to my own peace of mind. I am committed to holding myself in loving presence, even when I am challenged.

Figure 5: *Uttitha Hastasana* (Standing Mountain Pose with Arms Above)

GET CENTERED:
Phone Fight! The Anger-Sadness Cocktail

Breathe in deeply to bring your mind home to your body. Then look at or think of the person triggering this emotion: with mindfulness, you can see that she is unhappy, that she is suffering.

Thich Nhat Hanh

One of my tweens and I were having one of our regularly scheduled fights about her phone use. Texting, instagram, snapchat—all vehicles that basically pull her attention away from, in my humble opinion, more meaningful ways of connecting. The more I insisted and threatened that she "get off that phone", the more tenaciously she clung to it.

This week I demanded she surrender her phone to me, and when she didn't, I grabbed it out of her hands. We both yelled and screamed at each other, and it sucked. I won the phone, but it was far from a victory.

After dropping her off to school, I felt overwhelmed with anger. How could she be so defiant, I began to contemplate. I would never have acted this way with my mother, I told myself. Because she was at school, I had no choice but to sit with the feelings. I couldn't rehash it or resolve it with her. I breathed in and noticed that the anger was making my heart beat faster and my stomach feel nauseous. As I sat with this yuck, something else was lurking underneath it all.

The well of anger was replaced by swells of tears. It became clear in that moment that these angry struggles were primarily based on anxiety and sadness. Anxiety that she'll not enjoy deep relationships because snapchat exalts the superficial. Anxiety that my parenting probably is fiercely inadequate because this felt out of control. Worry that her life was going to fall off the tracks while I stood by, paying AT&T to strip her soul. Sadness that this wasn't how I envisioned her adolescent years. And sadness that her late tween/early teen years were being taken over by something that I, in an effort to keep her "connected", put in her very own precious hands.

Real anxieties, real sadness. It became clear to me that I was fighting not only my daughter but fighting my own feelings of loss about her growing up and my concerns that I wasn't being a "good mom."

When she came home from school, I must've surprised her by not getting into my typical rant about her phone. I told her how sad I was about fighting, and that I felt pained by her words. I apologized for hurting her feelings. I reasoned with her, explaining that being a teenager was new for her, and raising a teenager was new for me—exciting but really challenging at times. The armor that each of us had erected began to soften. "I'm sorry, Mommy. It's just I need my phone to see what my friends are doing." This time, I didn't lecture her on how much better it is to have face-to-face contact with people. I just listened. We talked for a long while, and though fruitful, it wasn't all flowers and pretty skies. When the unpleasant feelings came up, I let them and then listened internally.

I noticed where my muscles tightened, and my bones misaligned during this challenge. We all do this differently. For me, my shoulders round, my arms and neck tense up, my breath goes underground. Classic Fight, Flight, or Freeze response. So, I consciously told my upper body to relax and my spine to elongate as I took a deep breath in and a long exhale out. I did this for a good 30-45 seconds until my nervous system could hit the reset button.

The somewhat more "chill" state helped me avoid getting caught up in the "storyline." The storyline is the anxious questions like, "OMG, why is this happening?" or "if this going on now, what's the future going to hold?". You'll know you're in the middle of the storyline because it'll have you justifying, explaining, and most likely blaming yourself, your child, and even those not in the room. Though it's useful to figure out the whys, it's probably best not to do the exploration in the middle of agitation. When the heat is on, this is the time to let the emotions come up, label them ("angry," "sad"), and get a little distance from the swirling feelings so that you can return to the conversation at hand. This pausing in the middle of intense situations with our kids is so simple, and so amazingly helpful in getting us centered and clear.

These two techniques dovetail, making healthy inroads towards keeping our hearts open and receptive both to ourselves and to our kids. From a place of calmer clarity, we chatted about boundaries for her phone and developed a system that both she and I could live with. I'm not so unrealistic as to think that this will solve things, but it's a start, a work in progress. More important is that these tools can help us keep some sanity during those heated moments. By coming back to breath, to body signals, and going underneath the mental chatter, we stand a better chance at finding our internal peace instead of going to pieces.

HEALING YOGA POSE: *Balasana.* (Child's Pose). Kneel on your mat, placing the tops of your feet on the mat and bringing your big toes together behind you. Sit back so that your hips and gluteus are resting on or towards your heels. Separate your knees and then fold forward so that your upper body now rests between your legs. If your head doesn't reach the floor, then you can place a block, blanket or pillow under your head so that your neck can release. If this causes pressure on your knees, or your hips don't quite reach your heels, then place a blanket underneath your knees for support. Can you send your breath into your lower back, imaging the lower back and upper hips broadening and expanding so that your back body can relax down? Place your arms alongside your body comfortably so that you can drop more deeply into this restorative pose. Breathe here for at least 10 breaths.

BENEFITS: *A restorative pose that rests the body and mind. A forward fold (from the knees down), this pose is known for its anti-anxiety properties. Relaxes the lower back and stretches the muscles that support the spinal column.*

BE-KIND-TO-YOUR-MINDSPEAK: I allow my feelings to be known by me so that I can stay in each moment. I create space by listening to my heart, identifying physical tension, and breathing calmly.

Figure 6: *Balasana* (Child's Pose)

GET CENTERED:
Disconnect the Wires of
Your Panic Button

*The quality of difficulty, struggle, pain, dissatisfaction, or
unpleasantness will remind me to have the simple thought:
"Other people feel this." Now that may sound simplistic--
maybe not all that important. But, believe me, it makes a big
difference because the isolation, personal burden, loneliness, and
desperation of pain gets very strong. And you think you're the
only one. I've had people actually say to me, "I think no one else
in the world feels this kind of pain." And then I can say to them
with tremendous confidence: "You're wrong."*

Pema Chodron

The past several weeks, I've woken up with a feeling of panic. It could be
because the government is such a mess, my hormones are in an uprising of
their own, I'm living with three lively, awesome— did I mention lively?—
teens/tween girls, or for any number of reasons. But, for someone like
me, who usually wakes up in a peaceful state of mind, this unwelcome
panicky feeling was unnerving. My day was off-kilter before my feet got
out from under the covers.

That is, until this morning. I turned a corner. I used a variation of a
Tonglen Practice that substantially shifted things for the better—much
better—so I want to share it with you here.

The variation is very simple and goes like this: as I inhale, I imagine
breathing in all the amorphous panicky feeling that me and millions of
other people like me are experiencing around the globe. Other moms.
Dads, kids, people in all sorts of situations. For every single one of us.

Next, as I exhale, I imagine sending white healing light to all those,
including me, who are suffering with this panic/anxiety/stress. I repeated
this breathing cycle, pairing my inhale with a drawing in of all the panic
feelings and pairing my exhale with the sending out of robust white,
healing light to everyone who is panicky. I repeated it around 10 times,

until I was more in touch with feeling peaceful and grounded, feeling more like myself. I could literally feel the anxiety leaving my bones. I added a couple extra cycles for good measure. I felt so much lighter, it wasn't even funny.

I'm a mechanism-gal, and I want to know why the thing works. I don't really have an answer. As Pema Chodron reminds us, it may have something to do with recognizing that millions of other people feel this way too and we are not alone in it. Or perhaps it's because sending out healing white light to our fellow humans feels somehow healing. Or maybe it is simply because concentrated attention on our breath soothes the nervous system. As inspired by that owl in the tootsie roll lollipop commercial from back in the day, "the world may never know." But, I do know, this thing works. Why not give it a go next time you need it—for any difficult emotional space, even ones that are amorphous in nature but have you uneasy—this stuff is simply magic.

HEALING YOGA POSE: *Tonglen Meditation Practice.* This is a meditation to get you centered again. When a challenging emotion comes up, pause. Take a deep breath in, imagining drawing in the same emotion that millions of people world-wide are feeling. You can take in the energy through all the pores of your body, your skin, your hair, etc. Then, as you exhale, imagine sending out healing white light to all those who are struggling with the challenging emotion, as if your exhaled intention will offer them some kind of relief, too. Send out the compassionate loving healing energy through every pore of your body, transforming your experience from heaviness to lightness. Notice how you feel in your body after even just one cycle of breath of this. Repeat at least 10 more times, or until you feel grounded and centered again. You can do this as a regular daily practice, or even on-the-fly whenever a strong emotion comes up.

BENEFITS: *Quiets the mind, releases tension from the body. Relaxes the nervous system. Connects you to other humans in a deeply compassionate way.*

BE-KIND-TO-YOUR-MINDSPEAK: I belong to all others on this planet. I am a healer in ways big and small. I am centered in my bones. I can breathe again.

Figure 7: *Tonglen Meditation Practice*

GET CENTERED: DISCONNECT THE WIRES OF YOUR PANIC BUTTON

GET CENTERED:
Control Only What You Can

You don't want your happiness to be conditional upon the behavior of other people. It's hard enough to control ourselves.

Michael Singer

For a long time, I'd wake up many mornings to the following thoughts: "today is going to be a better day. Today, I will not fight with the kids, there'll be no screaming, and we will all go to bed at the end of the day feeling happy."

As it would happen, I'd often go to bed later that night with some sadness, anger, and regret because somewhere along the way, I lost it and things careened off the rails. Nothing cataclysmic, but just enough to make me feel like a bad mom. Truth is, there are days where we all feel crappy as moms, days where we want to pull our hair out and days where we've considered sucking down half a bottle of wine with lunch.

When we pan back and take a broader perspective on the situation— whether it's that they make a mess all over the house, ignore your suggestions to do homework, use electronic devices like they're going out of style, or whatever—it's clear that we can't control our children. In fact, the only thing we can really control in any situation, especially those involving other human beings—is our own attitude. That is, we control the way we relate to ourselves as we relate to whatever is going on. Annoying truth, I know.

Perhaps this major feature of parenting—that we actually can't "control" our children, especially as they get older—is by design. It's probably built into the system of parenting so that we are on target for raising independent and self-sufficient children.

What is easy to forget when we are in the trenches of parenting, is that feeling frustrated is an integral part of being an involved parent. It may not be what we post on Facebook or Instagram, but it's real nonetheless. And, the frustration is nothing to rail against, though there are days when it will bring us to our knees, to tears, or to both. So, how can we best relax with the ups and the downs of real parenting?

One of the key pieces to relaxing with your parenting is to notice how you react to yourself when you are feeling frustrated with your child. The focus, you might've picked up on, is not on them—it's on how you relate to you! Most of us respond to frustration by getting even more annoyed, even more impatient, even more aggravated. I've been there. But, adding more irritation to a frustrating situation is like trying to extinguish a fire by throwing a gallon of gasoline onto the fiery blaze (well, gas is a liquid, after all).

Relating to ourselves with more patience and more kindness (rather than relating to ourselves with more frustration) means paying attention to how our body feels. For instance, the next time you're in one of these situations, feel where your body is tensing up—jaw, throat, scalp, temples. This isn't difficult, but it seems to require a vigilant mindfulness to pull off. I guess you could even say it requires trusting the process. One great path to relating to ourselves with more kindness is to recognize our own vulnerability. Making the decision not to push yourself into a box, but instead to respect that you can have days where you feel off, and that these moments are also an integral part of the process of being a conscious and present parent.

HEALING YOGA POSE: *Viparita Virabhadrasana.* (Reverse Warrior Pose). Come into a Warrior II position, right foot forward. Spin your front palm to the sky and wrap your back arm around your low back. Drop your tailbone even heavier, bend more into the front knee, and let your arm reach up overhead, so your palm is facing towards the back of the room. Breathe into the ribs and right lung deeply, five breaths. Return to Warrior II and then switch sides.

BENEFITS: *Allows the intercostal section of the ribs to expand to accommodate more air. Increases lung capacity. Stretches side body laterally. Stretches inner thigh and armpit. Gently stimulates the adrenal glands. Increases oxygen to the brain and invigorates your mind.*

BE-KIND-TO-YOUR-MINDSPEAK: I listen with compassion and clarity. I act from a place of being centered and tender-hearted. Everyone moment offers me something to be grateful for.

Figure 8: *Viparita Virabhadrasan* (Reverse Warrior Pose)

GET CENTERED:
Feeling Off? Come Back Home to Your Wise Witness

Let everything happen to you: beauty and terror. Just keep going. No Feeling is Final.

Rainer Maria Rilke

Ever have one of those days where you just feel "off"?

I mean, everything is technically fine, everyone is where they belong, but something just doesn't feel right? I struggled with this recently. It is part and parcel of becoming more attuned to our internal awareness. Several years ago, I might've been feeling "off" but instead of working with it, I would've fought my way out of it, ate myself out of it, shopped myself out of it—perhaps you have had your own brand of how you deal with feeling "off." Thing is, as conscious-minded people, it is frustrating when we can't figure out what triggered the feeling of being "off." When I kept coming up empty on the reasoning, I decided to work on figuring out how to make peace with this challenging state as I got through the day. The answer might come, the answer might not; but in either case, I needed to be as present as possible to live my life.

To make peace with this amorphous feeling of being "off", I began by intentionally slowing down. I'm talking WAY down. Taking a moment to pause as things whirled around me. Yes, I continued with the carpool, the laundry, the homework helping, but I literally told myself to take each minute, breath by breath. To not get overwhelmed with all that has to be done, but to just be in this moment with this very breath.

Next, I let myself really feel the uncomfortableness, the uncertainty of the mood. It was not easy. I decided not to put on a happy face, or pull myself up by my bootstraps, but instead just got still. I decided I'd cultivate being still with this relatively annoying but painless feeling. Of course each moment—happy, sad, frustrating—well, they're all just temporary anyway. I felt my belly rise to receive each breath and fall as each breath left. My breath became like a metronome. This became an internal anchor to attach my consciousness onto. It also helped me recognize Rilke's words that "no feeling is final." I don't have to worry that this sensation will last forever, because I know that it actually will move through me and be replaced by another swirl of sensations and emotions. By surrounding my attachment to this peculiar emotional state, I could be more even-keeled and open to receive my children. This becomes the fundamental foundation of mindful parenting.

This little pause put me in a calmer state to begin to notice, who exactly was it that was noticing that I was not feeling centered?

There was some part of me, the part of me that represented some kind of wisdom, that was aware that I was feeling off. It was as if there were two parts of my mind—the part that says the thoughts and the part of me that knows that I'm having the thoughts. The part that knows we are having the thoughts is the witness. Sages have been talking about this phenomena for eons—but it was the first time I experientially connected to it. It was also the first time I didn't climb back into bed with the part of me thinking the thoughts, but instead stayed at the level of the witness.

So, while my thoughts were busy trying to figure out all the reasons why I wasn't feeling good, trying to run away from the feeling with various numbing agents, another part of me knew that I was feeling off and knew that the thoughts were not "me." This part is the witness of our consciousness.

I started to call this witness the Wiseness—a kind of hybrid between the "witness" that contemplative thinkers point to—and Your Highness, as I believe that this part of our mind embodies a wise nobleness. It is imbued with a certain stature that remains above the fray. It doesn't get itself caught up—it sits in its seat of nobility, at all times, and simply watches the mind. The Wiseness is the part of you that does not come and go itself but watches your mind's thoughts come and go. If the Wiseness came and went with your thoughts, then guess what? You'd go with your thoughts! But, you don't. We stay and we watch the thoughts as they come and go.

I noticed that the more in touch with the Wiseness I was, the more I began to embody the qualities of that centeredness. I had more and more space between my mind's incessant waves and the deeper reality of being a centered mom.

From the place of the Wiseness, I notice when I'm getting upset—maybe it's in response to a push-pull game launched by one of my teens—but it could be due to anything. It doesn't matter—what matters here is the noticing of the feelings. The noticing is the portal into the Wiseness. It puts us in a state of mind that is more relaxed and aware. Calmer, even. It's from here that we can experience what Rilke points to in his suggestion at the beginning of this blog that we should let in each and every feeling—happy, sad, frustrated, worried, or simply off—because they're all temporary anyway. It is the Wiseness that remains steady.

Repeatedly reminding ourselves to elevate our consciousness to the level of the Wiseness means we can live alongside the uncomfortable feelings that we all experience and watch them transform into the next set of emotions. In this way, we are not relying on any specific external event to keep us centered; we are operating from the place of the Wiseness. Wouldn't it be something if instead of trying to find our center, we simply embodied it?

HEALING YOGA POSE: *Utthita Parsvakonasana.* (Extended Side Angle Lunge Pose). Come into Warrior II with your right foot in front. With your right knee bent, lean forward and place your right elbow on your right thigh. Your right palm faces up to the sky. Put your left hand on your left hip bone and use it to gently spin your left ribs upward, drawing your right ribs towards the front of the room. Then, extend your left arm up to the ceiling, or reach your left arm over your head, with your left bicep over your left ear. You can stay here or drop your right hand to your ankle or to a block inside your right foot. For more advanced, wrap your left arm behind your torso so that it is in a yoga bind, shoulder externally rotated. Gaze over your left shoulder. Breathe for 10 breaths. Rise and then repeat with left foot forward.

BENEFITS: *Similar to the benefits of Warrior II with the added benefit of deepening the inner groin stretch and facilitating the opening of the hip flexor of the back leg. Slight twist aids digestion. Nourishes kidneys. Cultivates the feeling of being centered.*

BE-KIND-TO-YOUR-MINDSPEAK: I take each moment breath by breath. I flow with the moment and know that I am safe now.

Figure 9: *Utthita Parsvakonasana* (Extended Side Angle Lunge Pose)

GET CENTERED:
To My Friends Who Have Experienced Trauma as Children

Most of us have real anger and suffering living inside us. Perhaps in the past we were oppressed or mistreated, and all that pain is still right there, buried in our store consciousness. We haven't processed and transformed our relationship with what happened to us and we sit there alone with all that anger, hatred, despair and suffering. If we were abused when were young, every time our thinking mind goes back over that event, it's like we're experiencing the abuse all over again.

Thich Nhat Hahn

The #MeToo movement, including Dr. Ford's testimony on the Senate floor in 2018, was an eye-opener for many of us. Even though I personally had experienced sexual assault and figured others had too, I was not prepared for the staggering number of brave women and men who publicly came forward to share their experiences of pain and violation. I also wasn't prepared for the amazing feeling that this movement could actually change the climate that our daughters and sons grow up in.

By the time most of us reach adulthood, we have experienced some form of trauma, ranging from heartbreak to the more intense physical, sexual, and emotional abuses. Though the actual trauma may have been experienced decades ago, often there are hidden tender and hurting spaces in its wake. Healing is a lengthy process, even years after the event, things can happen that "trigger" a traumatic response. That is, current events in our lives that are not directly related to the trauma we experienced can evoke a reaction that is more intense than the situation at hand deserves. What happens when we are overreactive is that we are no longer in the present. However, by being aware of when we are triggered, and working on maintaining our calm and presence, we are, in fact, helping our children and ourselves.

Psychologists who study the long-reach of trauma will note that when your child enters the age that the parent was when they experienced a traumatic event, a deep part of them will relive the experience. This is beyond a simple remembering of the event—it is as if we're actually re-experiencing the trauma. This is critical to keep in mind so that we are not blind-sighted when the kids reach that age in which we experienced a significant loss or abuse.

I believe the human system is built this way so we can heal unresolved issues from our earlier wounding. It also may be a survival mechanism, in that our hyper vigilance helps us protect our children by warning them of dangers in their environment. However, like most automatic survival mechanisms, these processes can take on a life of their own. That is why it's critically important use these uncomfortable situations as opportunities to set the course for the next generation. To harness the hidden power in these circumstances by becoming aware of when you're triggered and before stepping into overreaction, use the trigger as a signal to get centered.

How do you know when you're triggered? For me, all of a sudden I feel overly anxious, overly angry, or conversely, like I want to withdraw and hide. I examine whether or not a real danger is evident. In nearly every single case of being triggered, there actually is no real danger (if there is, please address it immediately and maybe even get back up help). If there is no real danger, this is the critical moment. Breathing deeply and name feelings "worried, scared, agitated", can heal. Yes, it'll reduce the likelihood that you'll act from the wounded place, but it will also help you soothe the hurting places. As if you were a loving parent to yourself, nurturing and healing the wounded places. I've noticed that being kinder to myself reduces the likelihood that I'll act out from the painful residue of the trauma. It's an act of cultivating unconditional friendliness towards ourselves. We embrace the scared and vulnerable parts of ourselves, instead of pushing the challenging emotions away through reacting or overreacting.

When I am in a triggered phase (which when it is really bad, can last for most of a day and even span a couple days), I start my day by talking to the wounded little girl inside of me. I place a hand on my heart and on my abdomen (the Grounding Hand Posture), and I tell my younger selves (as I was abused as a young child and again as a young teenager), that I (the adult protectress) am here now. I comfort those wounded places within me with the knowledge that I am present and in charge, and that I will guide the hurt parts of myself with my mature wisdom, with strength and with kindness. By emotionally taking care of ourselves through tending the emotional wounds and anxieties, we are less likely to act from the painful residual trauma. And, we begin to remove the fear of our own emotions, which only serves to separate ourselves from ourselves and from those we love.

Use your triggers as an opportunity to deepen your friendship with yourself. Call upon your courage, which you likely have in spades. You'll be more connected to the reality of the present moment. This, in turn, will increase the likelihood that your actions will arise from the most centered part of you. Compassionately paying attention to ourselves has added benefits—of interrupting the transmission of trauma between generations, and of drawing any lingering shameful feelings out of the darkness and into the light. These earlier challenging experiences can become our opportunity to embrace ourselves with unconditional friendliness, to change the social climate that our children grow up in, and to powerfully reclaim our truth as we stand in solidarity.

HEALING YOGA POSE: *Eka Pada Rajakapotasana.* (One-Legged Half-Pigeon Pose). Come into Downward Dog. Move forward into plank position and pull your right knee towards your right elbow. Gently drop your right knee down towards your right wrist. Move your right ankle towards your left wrist (doesn't have to touch!). Flex your right toes. Your left knee is pointing down towards the floor, the top of your left foot is resting on the mat. Slowly lower both hips towards the floor and move your torso forward so that you are closer to the floor. Place your hands on the floor underneath your shoulders. Be mindful that you're not sending your hips over to the right, you'll want to keep them centered as much as possible here. If the floor is very far away from your right hip and buttock, place a blanket or block under it so that you can have more support. Now you can either keep your arms where they are or extend them out in front of you onto the floor. Rest here for at least ten breaths. Then return to Downward Dog and repeat on the left side.

BENEFITS: *Stretches the piriformis muscle and creates more flexibility in the external rotators of the hip. Opens the internal hip flexor of the leg extended behind you.*

BE-KIND-TO-YOUR-MINDSPEAK: I embrace myself, my history, and my life with unconditional friendliness. I am centered and safe.

Figure 10: *Eka Pada Rajakapotasana* (One-Legged Half-Pigeon Pose)

GET CENTERED:
When You Don't Feel Like a Good Mom

What she did have, after raising two children, was the equivalent of a PhD in mothering and my undying respect.

Barbara Delinsky

The MYTH.

The "good" mother never gets angry. She calmly states what she wants and manages to maintain her cool, no matter what.

The "good" mother has all the right answers at all times, even if those questions have baffled parents and philosophers alike for centuries.

The "good" mother can foresee when her child might be in danger, has her finger on the pulse of any trouble brewing, and easily and convincingly circumvents any problems.

The "good" mother strikes the balance between pushing her child (you know, developing grit) and soothing her child. She does this every time, ease and grace by her side.

The "good" mother has boundless patience, endless energy, and a perfectly pleasing disposition.

Her house, immaculate.

And her legs are always shaved.

Ahem. That isn't a "good" mother. That's a perfect mother. And **that! That** doesn't exist.

THE TRUTH.

In this era of hidden truths coming to light, let's add to the chopping block the "Good" Mother. Built on fantasy, she harbors a specific kind of destruction. It's one that traps us in an emotional straight jacket and blames us for just being human. It encourages us to think we're failing at this mom thing, even though we are doing more than a decent job.

A legit mom is far more real. Legit mom kisses scraped knees or comforts hurt feelings and has moments of freaking out and yelling at the kids. Legit mom holds her kid's hair back when he is throwing up, but sometimes says the wrong thing. Legit mom makes thousands of meals every year, and still can be driven to distraction. Legit mom spends countless hours driving her kids to various activities, worries about them on a regular basis, and also spaces out when they're explaining every detail of their entire day.

Legit mom doesn't have it all figured out, doesn't have all the answers or even all the right questions. She makes mistakes. She has doubts, worries, and pain—and yet, she opens her heart time after time. She gives herself enough emotional and psychological bandwidth to get angry, to feel anxious, and still to pick up the pieces so that she continues learning and growing herself.

Legit mom has enough space to let her children falter—and even fall—knowing that they are resilient. Legit mom welcomes her kids' expression of their own individual fingerprint but recognizes that relaxing with their self-expression is not for the faint of heart.

Legit mom finds a way to forgive herself, her children, and her family for being less than perfect. For she knows that it is in those precisely flawed places that the most vibrant pulsations of life live. The light only shines through the cracks, to paraphrase Leonard Cohen. Legit mom knows that staying in touch with the deeper reality of the stuck and the irritated will offer more breathing room for love, energy, and joy. She gives herself the courage to recognize her vulnerabilities and from there, writes her own story of keeping it real. Here's to us, too legit to quit.

HEALING YOGA POSE: *Skandasana* (Forward Fold Pose with Variation). Stand with your feet about three-four feet away from each other. Place your hands on your hips and engage your core. Bend both knees slightly as you lower your torso horizontally to hip height. Now bend your right knee deeply while shifting your hips over to the right. Straighten your left knee so that you can feel the stretch through the inner thigh of the left leg. You can put your hands to the floor for support. Take 5-10 breaths here. Then switch sides. After completing the second side, you can move freely back and forth between sides, exhaling into each side, and inhaling to come back to center.

BENEFITS: *Lengthens inner adductors, hamstrings, and stretches inner and outer hips. Improves core strength and balance while offering mental and emotional empowerment.*

BE-KIND-TO-YOUR-MINDSPEAK: I integrate my light with my darkness. I am strength and I am vulnerable. I know my personal truth and embrace myself at a deep level.

Figure 11: *Skandasana* (Forward Fold Pose with Variation)

GET BALANCED

Have you ever noticed that when we feel shaky in a balancing pose, our mind goes directly to that lack of steadiness, that wobble, that "Oh, crap, I'm gonna fall" thinking? Ironic, because by drawing our minds to the wobble, we often are thrown even further off-balance. This is not unlike what happens off the mat when we are feeling off-kilter. It is not the initial imbalance that causes the problem—have you noticed it's actually your reaction to the imbalance that creates the true instability? Here you go, a section that includes useful insights on how we throw ourselves off-balance and creative solutions for getting ourselves back to balance, every time.

GET BALANCED:
Steady That Bow

When you recover or discover something that nourishes your soul and brings joy, care enough about yourself to make room for it in your life.

Jean Shinoda Bolen

For years, I've believed that if I'm doing a good job as mom, then my kids will be shining examples of great young people. They won't complain about the food I make, will help those less fortunate, and will not get seduced by electronics. You know, they'd be a living-breathing-walking reflection of my great parenting skills.

Ahhh, doesn't work this way. As moms, we can do all the "right things" and still the response we get from our children may veer dramatically from what we had in mind. I'm reminded of this every time one of my lovelies slams her bedroom door in disgust. Or when something pops from one of their mouths that stops me dead in my tracks.

Maybe it's a good sign that I'm witnessing the health described in Damour's *Untangled* regarding adolescent girls: "instead of being rude or aggressive towards peers or teachers at school, she contains her irritation and waits until she is safely in your company to express it." A healthy sign maybe, but that doesn't stop it from being painful. Part of the pain is that, on an essential level, we can buy into the belief that we're responsible for their behavior and that their behavior reflects our worth as women and mothers.

Truth is, we are fundamentally *not* responsible for their behavior. The system was not designed so we could control anyone's behavior, especially as they grow and gain more independence. This is not some personal failing of you as a mom, our current society, the leadership in the country, or the internet. Since birth, these amazing and challenging people have had their own relationships to themselves, to their world, and even to God. When I recognized this, it helped stop me from banging my head against the wall in frustration. I do my best to guide, I stay committed to the process, but then I must let go of the outcome or I will lose my mind.

You know, you can flip the coin and realize we're not even responsible for their impressive talents or solid table manners. This may be even harder to accept, because it feels like our efforts at shaping them are paying off. But Kahlil Gibran reminds us, "You are the bows from which your children as living arrows are sent forth." The bow. Not the arrow. Not even the archer. Gibran goes on to add that "He [God] loves also the bow that is stable." I take from his wise words that our primary job as parents is just to steady the structure of that bow.

When a bow is stable, the arrows can be propelled with greater purpose and grace. Because we are sturdier, we become reliable and trustworthy and our beautiful arrows can access their own inner GPS. And guess what else? When we are steady, we are less likely to drive ourselves up the wall in the process of helping them fly. This philosophy becomes an extremely powerful antidote to the sinking feeling that you can't control where the arrow goes: you weren't meant to. You were meant to steady *your bow*.

How best to do that? How about a soulful yoga class, a massage, a date with your spouse, decadent chocolate, or singing like you're auditioning for The Voice? Whatever it is, let it be some activity that takes the stress down at least a few notches. And if you feel guilty doing what one of my neighbors calls "indulging," remember that research shows that being stressed impairs our cognitive functioning and increases inflammation. So, isn't it in everyone's best interests if our efforts were geared toward clarifying our minds, calming our bodies, and therefore steadying our bow?

When our focus is on how to make that bow steadier, how to make it more reliably trustworthy, then we don't put pressure on our children to make us feel successful at this parenting gig. They get to do their thing and we get to do ours. That attitude translates to a more relaxed feel in your body and in your home—and that vibe in itself is amazingly nurturing for everyone. It's accurate to say that the better you are at caring for yourself, the more reserves you'll have when caring for those you love. Steady your bow, and the world smiles.

HEALING YOGA POSE: *Virabhadrasana I.* (Warrior I Pose). Come into a lunge with your right foot forward and your left leg extended behind you, ball of foot pressing into the mat. Next, drop your left foot to the floor so that it is essentially pointing towards the front left corner of your mat. Bend your right knee so it rests above your ankle. Press the outer edge of your back foot into the mat. Draw your arms up towards the sky, palms can face each other over your head; more advanced, join palms over your head. Can you sink deeper into your front knee so that your knee is at a right angle and parallel to the floor? Take five to ten full breaths here and then repeat this pose on the other side.

BENEFITS: *Tones shoulders, arms, back. Increases openness in your chest and lungs. Improves balance and stability. Improves levels of energy. Feels empowering.*

BE-KIND-TO-YOUR-MINDSPEAK: I honor my body by listening deeply to my heart. I steady myself through kind actions towards myself. I reveal my compassionate and wise nature. By being present and steady, I relax.

Figure 12: *Virabhadrasana I* (Warrior I Pose)

GET BALANCED:
Love the Wobble

Balance is not something you find, it's something you create.

Jana Kingsford

Ever notice that when the competing demands of mothering, marriage, or work pull us in a million directions, we can feel seriously out of balance? Or when we are in an intense battle with one of our kids about some hot-button issue—and the feeling of shakiness is palpable. Much of the time, the anxiety around the wobble makes us wish the wobble wasn't even there. We resist the wobble. The resistance can take the form of over-shopping, over-consuming, overusing the internet, and even berating ourselves for feeling the way we feel. Though initially these efforts feel worthwhile (because they cover over the anxiety with something "to do" or at the least, something numbing), we all know that they actually don't work. In fact, most of us feel worse after we react to reduce the wobble. The steadiness we crave and deserve is further out of reach.

So, when the shakiness arises, here are a few ways to manage the stress of the wobble. First, notice it's there, and notice the temptation to act—either with negative self-chatter or actions that ultimately aren't supportive of your highest good—and then draw a big breath in. Slowly exhale the breath out. The wobble infuses the moment with anxiety, and deep breathing is an excellent way to help quell the overactive nervous system.

Second, redefine what the wobble means to you. Typically, the wobble is seen as a harbinger of bad things to come. It's why we resist it. But, if we remember that the wobble is part of the territory, in fact, it's a mini course correction, then we can relax more with it. It won't be the end of the world to see the wobble, we won't need to push it away, instead we can find the inner space to let go into the shakiness. By loving the wobble instead of resisting it, we are less likely to exacerbate the unsteadiness and more likely to re-stabilize ourselves. And, if we do happen to fall, we find more grace to get back up.

Embracing the wobble means that you trust yourself enough to be in process, to not be a finished product. It means that you find ways to celebrate the imperfections, including the shakiness. We won't cover up the shakiness but will use its presence to breathe more deeply and peek our curiosity about how to best support ourselves—for real this time. You'll have less rigidity, more playfulness, and more forgiveness—all by-products of loving the wobble.

HEALING YOGA POSE: *Vrikshasana* (Tree Pose). Stand on your right leg and place your left foot on your right inner calf, or thigh. Be careful not to push your left foot into the knee. Once you feel somewhat steady, go ahead and gently press the sole of your left foot into your standing leg. At the same time, press your right leg into the sole of your left foot. Can you feel how this creates a circuit of energy, with foot pressing into leg and leg pressing back into the sole of the foot? Keep your arms in prayer position at your heart center, or more advanced, raise arms above your head into a "V" shape. Find a drishti (i.e., a gaze point ahead of you) to help support your balance. (If this feels too advanced, place your left toes on the ground and press your left heel against the side of your right calf). Five to 10 breaths here, and then switch legs.

BENEFITS: *Improves balance. Enhances strength in legs, feet and opens hip flexor laterally. Cultivates greater concentration and ease. Releases tension in hips, strengthens arms.*

BE-KIND-TO-YOUR-MINDSPEAK: When the wobble shows up, I send this course correction some love. I am open to my inner experience. I relax in my own skin and trust the process today. I love the wobble.

Figure 13: *Vrikshasana* (Tree Pose)

GET BALANCED:
Be the Eye in the Storm

The cyclone derives its power from a calm center. So does a person.

Norman Vincent Peale

When I was a kid, my parents owned The Derby Diner Restaurant in northern New Jersey. During the height of the lunch and dinner rush, every seat was full, and lines of hungry customers looped around the building. Everyone, from the kitchen to the front of the house staff, was working full-tilt. Right in the middle of those stressful times, my Dad, the Head Chef, would be known to calmly walk out of the kitchen, sit on the back steps of the restaurant, and sip a cup of coffee.

Rather than join the frenzy of the kitchen crazies, Dad would take a moment to breathe and center himself. Though he might've been out there for just two minutes, it was all he needed to clear his head and ready himself to re-enter the buzz. He called this little respite in the middle of the craziness, "Abdul-time."

In that moment, most people didn't understand what he was doing. In fact, they might've been miffed that he left the kitchen when things were getting a little off the rails. Looking back now, it's clear that smack dab in the middle of the chaos, Dad was finding ground. He was centering himself, coming home. When he returned to the kitchen a few minutes later, he was peaceful and ready to tackle the next set of challenges. Perhaps the secret to his special sauce could be found in those moments where finding center was more important than managing the sails in an unwieldy storm.

The wisdom in his quiet action begs the question—when things are nuts in our homes, is it in our best interest to jump into the fray, or would it be more constructive and even kinder if we took a mini-break? This could be a moment of respite to consciously breath, to simply breathe fresh air, or to take the dog for a walk. Obviously, if taking a break would put your child in harm's way, don't do it. But, the vast majority of the time, we have the freedom to extract ourselves for a few moments. What prevents us from doing so? Maybe it's the belief that staying in the storm will improve things. Perhaps it is just the intensity, which can be alluring and addictive. We worry that we are conveying that we are weak or not committed. Actually, though, taking a mini-break represents us finding our inner strength and grounding.

I imagine that we've all had instances where we've stayed in an intense situation for a few minutes too long—and are well aware that it doesn't always put us in the most resourceful state. In fact, it can often lead to escalating things, and then guilt for not managing it differently. But, when you think about those who contribute the most wisely to a situation, it usually is the centered person. Relaxing your nervous system—*especially* in the middle of the storm—is really important. For example, if you and your child are having a heated argument that is getting nowhere, this is the time for us to excuse ourselves and disengage for a couple of minutes to regain our composure. After all, when they were younger, we tell our children to take "a time-out" or to go to their rooms. Now we are giving ourselves a 30-second time-out so that we can find calm before frustration gets the better of us. I let them know that I'm disengaging— and if possible—do it in a neutral way—rather than leaving in a huff or tears. This way, self-care of mama isn't perceived as punishment.

Taking a mini-break may just prevent us from having a mini-breakdown. It lets us sip peace of mind and sanity, and that invites us to broaden our perspective. In addition, it helps reduce the intensity of the situation. Do it when you need it, do it before you need it. If it makes you more available and puts you in a more resourceful state, I can't imagine a saner or more loving way to relate to your children than taking your own personal mini-break.

HEALING YOGA POSE: *Paschimottanasana.* (Seated Forward Fold Pose). Sit on your mat, extending both of your legs out in front of you. Flex your feet, so your toes pull back towards your knees. Lift both arms over head and draw a deep breath in. As you exhale, forward fold over your legs. If your back rounds significantly, place a blanket underneath your sitting bones and place a yoga strap around the soles of your feet, holding onto it with your hands. This will help your spine stay long as you bend from your hips. Engage your thigh muscles so your hamstrings can let go. Take 5-10 breaths here. Then sit back upright and shake out your legs. You can follow this with seated Cobbler's Pose, drawing the soles of your feet together, knees out to the side.

BENEFITS: *Improves energy by lengthening the spine. Soothes the nervous system. Stretches hamstrings, neck and entire back body. Calming, anti-anxiety pose.*

BE-KIND-TO-YOUR-MINDSPEAK: Today, I take time to nurture myself in both large and small ways. I cherish this moment and know that by staying connected to gratitude, I broaden my perspective, deepen my courage, and stay as centered as possible.

Figure 14: *Paschimottanasana* (Seated Forward Fold Pose)

GET BALANCED:
What Are You Feeding
Your Head?

We waste our precious energies trying to avoid loss when these energies should be applied to living.

Terry Cole-Whittaker

The national and global events of the past year have been intense—dangerous decisions coming from the White House, sexual abuse of the vulnerable by those in power, massive hurricanes, and mass shootings. It's enough to put even the most mindful of us into a tailspin. Intently focusing on recent events sets us up to be distracted, unavailable, and irritable with our children and families. The media's "High Alert" messaging can wreak havoc on our nervous system and leave us less emotional bandwidth to parent from. We can be worried and angry, which means that when typical frustrating mothering stuff comes up, we may be set up to overreact. How could we not? And how can we reclaim our internal power over our own thoughts and homes when the world is figuratively (and literally) on fire?

For starters, it's a good idea to just pause and witness how the emotional impact of what is going on in the world impacts your mind. Recognizing the feelings that are left in the wake of learning about events is an important step in setting emotional boundaries and taking responsible care of ourselves. Breathe into them, name them, and let them clear out of your system before interacting with your kids.

At the time of this writing (April 17, 2018), the news sources are talking about possible war with Syria, a president who has likely, with the help of Russia, interfered with elections, and impending trouble in the global markets. If I don't acknowledge the feelings of helplessness, anger, and fear that are present in my psyche, I'm doing myself and my kids a disservice. Not acknowledging the impact on our minds seems to truly stack the deck against our attempts at mindful mothering. Worrying about the world sets us up to feel overwhelmed, and then the typical frustrating aspects of parenting can take on greater weight—the carpooling, sibling conflicts, setting limits on stuff, can all get infused with the insanity that is going on in Washington and beyond.

The second key to responsibly taking in the media is to set boundaries around how much and when you consume media. I was kind of blown away when I did this. At certain points in the year, I was aware that I was ingesting several hours of news a day, eating up the media on-line, social media from friends, listening to the news radio when driving around town. This level of media consumption disrupted my capacity to be as emotionally available to my kids as I strive to be. So, I went on a little detox. For a few weeks, I simply skimmed the headlines, instead of reading all the nitty-gritty specifics. This way, I was in the know but because I'm not working for the Justice Department, or the Defense Department, or the media itself, I probably don't need to have our finger on the pulse of every machination that is going on.

Relatedly, take a peek at when in the day you absorb the news. I was a right before bedtime news reader (on my ever-present iPhone), and a first thing in the morning reader (again, thanks iPhone). I would take it in before I left the house for the day, and throughout the day as I drove to drop off and pick up my kids. This constant diet of media was like taking in too much sugar—at first, not so bad, but before long, you feel sick and kind of gross. So, I had to shift something. I began a different practice to bookend my days. I put an inspirational book (okay, ten inspirational books) on my bedside table. My favorite go-to people are Thich Nhat Hahn, Pema Chodron, Eva Pierrakos, and Tara Brach. Maybe this book you're holding might make it to your bedside (my fingers are crossed). Anyway, by preparing the reading before bedtime, it provided the easy access I needed so I'd turn to it. Ingesting calming and centering messages is seriously grounding, so why not turn to the calming presence of some thoughtful folks in those tender hours of the night or day? I've found that setting boundaries around consumption of media, though simple, can profoundly reorient our day, offers more room for hope and genuine empowerment.

Setting boundaries around consumption of media, though simple, can profoundly reorient your day. It helps deepen your feeling of being home in your own bodies. It leaves room for you to decompress. This, in turn, parlays into a more grounded and centered mom. Can you imagine how putting media in its place may help increase your being present with your kids?

The message really is to be aware, but not consumed. Protest, petition, write letters and checks, but in the end game, put media in its place. Notice when you take in the news what it does to your emotional equilibrium and recalibrate it so that you can be most present with your children in any given moment.

HEALING YOGA POSE: *Parvitta Utkatasana.* (Twisting Chair Pose). Place your feet hip-width distance apart. Place your hands at your heart in prayer position. Draw your sitting bones back behind you, so you are basically sitting in the air, hips no lower than knee height. Strongly pull in your abdominal core. Draw in a full breath and as you exhale, twist your left elbow past your right thigh. Breathe in this position for at least 7-10 breaths. Relax any tension in your face or jaw. To come out of this pose, move your torso and elbows back through center, as you forward fold. Release your hands down to the floor or keep them at the back of your head. Take five full cycles of breath in the forward fold, with knees slightly bent. Then, sit back into the chair pose and twist to your other side on an exhale. When completed with this second twist, forward fold for at least ten breaths. Rest.

BENEFITS: *Strengthens the quadriceps, hamstrings, abdominal core and shoulders. Opens the hip flexor of the back leg. Improves breathing capacity. Enhances balance. Aids in digestion and releasing tension along the sides of the body. Releases emotional stress.*

BE-KIND-TO-YOUR-MINDSPEAK: I focus my energy on the situations that I can control. I know that everything is happening for the highest good of all concerned and I trust in the process. I stand as a warrior of strength and surrender.

Figure 15: *Parvitta Utkatasana* (Twisting Chair Pose)

GET BALANCED:
What Else Could This Mean?

There is no stress. It is a misinterpretation of a situation. Just change your perception and the stress will melt away.

Debasish Mridha

On a beautiful summer day, I took the children, our dog Baci, and a picnic lunch to the Brookline Reservoir. The sun was shining, the geese were flocking, and we were enjoying the beauty of the water together. Well, all that was about to change.

Serenity was instantly shattered when Baci spotted, sitting right on the water's edge, a vicious-looking coyote. The coyote's head was down, teeth bared, eyes wide open and body stiffened. Baci's low rumble turned into massive action, rapidly pulling the leash and me toward this beast.

Baci was in full fight/flight mode and so was I. My chest and neck tensed with adrenaline and my sweating hand began to slip off his leash. As we charged closer, I noticed something strange about this coyote. It was still. Very still. As in 'made of rubber' still. A coyote statue that someone had staked into the ground.

Relieved. Deep breaths. And recognition—our lives are like this. Somedays, a lot like this. Misreading a situation, interpreting danger when things are safe, thinking someone said or did something hurtful when in fact nothing of the kind happened. Even my car does this when I put my purse in the front passenger seat. The seatbelt sign goes on and the bell rings relentlessly as if an unbuckled person was in that seat—though actually, no one is there.

As Shannon L. Alder reminds us, "most misunderstandings in the world could be avoided if people would simply take the time to ask, 'What else could this mean?'" A simple and profound question. In fact, it's brilliant because not only does it encourage inquisitiveness, but it puts space between the situation and our thoughts. It interrupts the train of thinking that sees something, creates a story about it, and boom, sends us off and running, full-on stress reaction. In that interrupted space, we can regroup, gather more information, and respond from a place of being grounded.

What else could this mean? This type of curiosity in our relationships may help us see with more clarity, whether it's to better understand an ambiguous look from our tween, a confusing message from a loved one, or a complicated circumstance. Check out what happens when you interrupt the "story" in your head with this inquiry. Rather than getting caught up in believing something that might not be true, this query asks us to reflect on the events and our reactions to the events. The brain has been known to perceive things that actually aren't there—and it's kind of embarrassing. Sometimes, we can think that our child is being less than kind, when in fact, nothing of the sort has happened. By pausing and taking a deep breath into this inquiry, we contribute to a saner world.

Today, would you join me in asking, "what else could this mean" when your defenses reach for the panic button? I believe that doing so will foster an atmosphere of greater trust and well-being. Even if something is wrong, you are then poised to deal with it from inquisitiveness and openness, instead of judgement.

HEALING YOGA POSE: *Nataragasana.* (Dancer's Pose). Start in Standing Mountain Pose with your arms stretched over your head. Now shift your weight onto your right foot and bend your left knee so that your left foot is behind you. Turn your left arm towards the left wall, so your palm is spinning out towards the wall. Take hold of the inside of your left foot—right at the arch of the foot—with your left palm. Lengthen your left leg behind you, holding onto the left foot with your left hand (Don't expect your left leg to go straight behind you here! It's more about the extension of the leg). Doing this will pull your torso forward, allowing you to approximate a standing backbend. Extend your right arm forward so that it is higher than shoulder height. Gaze straight ahead for 10 breaths. Deepen each breath as you come more fully into the pose. Release the pose, standing with both feet on the ground, hands alongside you. Take a full cycle of breath and then switch sides.

BENEFITS: *Strengthens your standing leg. Opens the hip flexors and groins of lifted leg. Releases tension in shoulders and front of the chest; strengthens the biceps and triceps of the arm reaching forward. Backbend draws spine into its natural arch and contributes to lifting your mood. Helps lift depression.*

BE-KIND-TO-YOUR-MINDSPEAK: I am open and curious. My world is now safe. I trust this moment. I communicate effectively with those closest to me. I am patient and hopeful.

Figure 16: *Nataragasana* (Dancer's Pose)

GET BALANCED:
The Art of Receiving

Refusing to receive leaves us chronically empty, prone to addiction, obsession, codependency, or an external psychological hunger that's never quite satisfied. The healthy alternative is to stop merely closing down and learn to receive wisely, fully accepting good gifts without being damaged by bad ones. The secret is this: No matter what happens, keep your heart open.

Martha Beck

This year, I watched as each of my children tore into their Christmas gifts with glee. They were deeply absorbed in each gift: present, aware, grateful. Remember those days when it was easy to receive with joy? Lately, though, receiving can become more elusive, more freighted. It extends not just to material goods, but to those intangibles that we all crave but sometimes push away—love, recognition, admiration. Though the old adage would say, it's better to give than to receive, I truly wonder about the validity of that statement. Is it really better to give than receive? Perhaps the saying was touted as a way to encourage some of us to be more generous, but many of us mamas give way too much, and never fully let ourselves receive—often not even a compliment! It's probably clear to each of us that when we don't really let ourselves relax enough to receive, we can wind up feeling depleted and even resentful.

In order to shift anything internally, it's useful to consider what good comes from not receiving? To name a few, when we don't let ourselves receive, we don't have to deal with the anxiety around whether or not we deserve the goodies, whether it's too much, whether we are worthy of it. Relatedly, by not receiving we don't have to worry about whether we are on the hook to give back. Finally, by primarily giving and not receiving, we stay in control of the situation. Many years ago I had a friend who would only give and would consistently refuse any of my efforts of generosity; after a while, it took on a kind of hostile holding tone, and her unwillingness to participate in the flow of give and take in the friendship ultimately contributed to its decline. Something stirred deep within me that indicated things were out of balance and just not authentic.

In fact, I've begun to think that withholding from receiving life's pleasures might actually be worse than not giving anything to anyone. When we don't open ourselves up to the give and take, we literally and figuratively fall out of balance. As mothers, this sets us up for poor overall health (mental, physical, spiritual, emotional), and it robs our kids from the opportunity of seeing us enjoy the pleasures of life.

Looking at nature, we know that there is a gracious interplay between giving and receiving. The earth humbly receives the rainfall that allows the soil and oceans to continue to thrive. We receive sunlight in the day and moonlight in the evening. It's as if giving and receiving are harmonious dance partners—one can't exist without the other. Implicit within this healthy relationship between give and take is a good dose of humility. So, the question for many of us is, if we want to be more receptive, how would we go about getting out of our own way?

I've been thinking about the capacity to receive as if we each had our own personal receptivity valve. Like any physical structure, if that valve is tense and tight, not much can get through. If the valve is relaxed, it easily takes in what it needs and recognizes when it's satisfied. Our job is perhaps to know when and how to relax so we can allow the valve to open. I've been playing with a three-pronged approach lately in regard to this and I've found it really helps. The first prong is inspired by Oprah, who says, "I finally had to stop and consider what I believe is one of the most important questions a woman can ask herself: What do I really want—and what is my spirit telling me is the best way to proceed?"

To articulate a mature and honest answer, it may be necessary to get quiet, almost in a meditative state. Close your eyes and imagine you are surrounded by a warm golden healing light, like a vibrant shimmering egg that envelopes your physical body. From this space, ask yourself, what do you really want? Be open to images that might pop up, words, sensations and then like Hansel and Gretel following the breadcrumbs home, let these imaginings bring you to an inner home that is safe and nourishing. If anxiety pops up, ask it to relax along with you as you hear your answers from within. In addition to giving you an answer that may increase your feeling of being understood and cherished, this approach allows you to fine-tune your inner intuition. The answers I tend to get from this mental place always make sense.

For instance, when my children were very little, I definitely craved more solitude. That is me receiving me, or me receiving God. At other points in my life, it's been a night out with my husband, or hanging out with dear friends. Sometimes it's that I need more exercise, and sometimes, I need more rest. I once signed up for an acting class because I felt that was what my wise higher-self needed in order to get filled up. This is a type of receiving. Asking for an answer, waiting for the response, and then taking action with respect to the message.

For many of us anxiety will be a consistent feature of receiving. Typically, when anxiety shows up, we tense around it, prepping for something negative to happen. This shuts down the receptivity valve—and neuroscience shows us that when we are anxious, we literally prevent access to our brain's pleasure center.

So, what can we do? One path is to change the relationship you have with the anxiety. When anxiety comes up, recognize it either as a thought or a feeling and examine whether there is any real validity to it. If it's relevant, attend to whatever is present (e.g., if I let them take my daughter to soccer, I always notice I feel obliged to XYZ in return). Sometimes there is an implicit contract in place, and we understandably would rather not be involved in that exchange. This is a valid concern and being aware of the expectations help to diffuse the anxiety.

In many cases, however, the anxiety shows up because it thinks it's protecting us from something, even if in actuality there is nothing that needs to be safeguarded against. It may be that anxiety is there because something from the past got triggered, maybe even partly because of past traumas, or even issues of worthiness. The Zen tradition would have us recognize the anxiety is present, call it by name, and then bring our attention back to the present moment. You can do this best by taking full and deep inhales and exhales.

The final step in this process is to explore gratitude. Of course, it's great to express gratitude toward the gift-bearer. But gratitude that is really life-sustaining is the appreciation towards God or Source Energy. Thanking God for the people in your life, for your capacity to be present, for your willingness to engage in a process of surrender which ultimately brings creative growth and spiritual evolution.

Try this three-pronged approach the next time you are feeling a tightness in your capacity to receive. First, become attuned to what you want for yourself. Second, notice if anxious thoughts or feelings are present, label it "anxious thinking," and use deep breathing to soothe your nervous system. Third, offer gratitude for being on this path of unfolding growth and for the wonderful people/events/experiences in your world. Through this three-pronged approach, you position yourself to keep your receptivity valve open and relaxed.

HEALING YOGA POSE: *Baddha Virabhadrasana.* (Humble Warrior Pose). Come into Warrior I with your lower body, right foot forward, the toes of your back foot facing the top left corner of your mat. Clasp your hands behind your low back, pushing one shoulder blade, and then the other into your back. With a straight spine and a long exhale, lean forward so your right shoulder moves towards the inside of your right knee. With your head relaxed down, allow your interlaced hands to move forward over you, towards the front of the room. Pull your right hip back gently, in the direction of your right heel. Do you notice how your shoulders are stretching and your right hip is working hard to stabilize you here? Take 10 deep breaths into your pose. Slowly come back up to starting position and repeat on other side.

BENEFITS: *Strengthens front thigh, hip, and butt. Loosens tight shoulders. Relaxes the mind. Opens hip of the back leg. Head lower to the ground can help soothe an overactive nervous system.*

BE-KIND-TO-YOUR-MINDSPEAK: I let life flow through me. I offer my best to this world, and thus I am aligned with my highest good. Every day, it's easier for me to give and to take with joy.

Figure 17: *Baddha Virabhadrasana* (Humble Warrior Pose)

GET BALANCED:
Love Yourself As You Love Your Neighbor

You can be the most beautiful person in the world and everybody sees light and rainbows when they look at you, but if you yourself don't know it, all of that doesn't even matter. Every second that you spend on doubting your worth, every moment that you use to criticize yourself, is a second of your life wasted, is a moment of your life thrown away. It's not like you have forever, so don't waste any of your seconds, don't throw even one of your moments away.

C. JoyBell

We've all heard the expression "Love your neighbor as you love yourself." Funny because in many circumstances, we don't even give ourselves the love we deserve. A truly radical suggestion is to love OURSELVES as we love our neighbors/children/partners/pets. It's quite likely that you love everyone else in your life with a fierceness and dedication that is undeniable. So, it's in you already. It's just a matter of redistributing that light so that some of its golden rays shine onto you, too.

When it comes to giving generously to ourselves, I'm sorry to report that many of us can easily become stingy misers. Have you ever turned a blind eye to your own exhaustion, and pushed it into overdrive? I know I have. As mothers, it's almost expected of us. You may help everyone around you, but if you collapse regularly into bed, into that second glass of wine, or into an emotional heap, then why not take a minute to reevaluate how you allocate your energetic resources?

I've seen this in myself and in many of my friends. When depletion becomes our habit, we set ourselves up for a bumpier than necessary ride. In these circumstances, it's time to switch gears or we'll risk resentment or burn out. Because when we are depleted, it's as if our unfed spiritual self is on high alert. Rather than being in the present moment, a deep part of us is looking and searching for something else. This diminishes our capacity to enjoy our children, or to relax with the happiness that already is here.

From time to time, taking an honest look at where you fall on the priority list is important. The dominant culture would have us put ourselves at the bottom of the list—after all, we are MOTHERS. But, we need to update the definition of what it means to be a mother. We are at a critical point in our culture where motherhood no longer needs be defined by those adults who aren't currently mothering, and who aren't rolling up their sleeves to work alongside us. A motherhood that may have worked in the past might really hurt us and our children in the present. We must define the narrative of motherhood by those of us who are awake, those of us who are actually in the trenches mothering, those of us who value self-compassion. This is the only sane path to a healthy experience of parenthood today.

Buying into the societal messages that our needs belong at the bottom of the list, after everyone else, is a 1950s recipe that will have us dragging through the day and resentful at night. Delegating and reorganizing things so we don't drive ourselves into the ground is necessary. It's real. It's honest. And it takes courage.

Sometimes the straitjacket is tightened not just by society at large, but by other well-meaning moms. Over the last several years, I've gotten pretty good with the "That sounds like such an interesting opportunity (if it does), and I'm already committed. I can't help this time." I'll tell you, it's not easy at first. I used to feel like a fish that got dumped out of its bowl the first few times I said this. Yet, I'm getting better at it, and even working on not saying "I'm sorry." Because, like that old PeeWee Herman movie, I'm not sorry at all! I'm taking care of myself and this is an important boundary to establish.

If this still feels difficult to imagine, take the following scenario: Your good friend is stressed out and anxious. The demands on her energy are overwhelming and she is flipping out, looking for help. Which of these options best describes how you'd respond? Option A: Berate her. Tell her she can't handle this, and it was ridiculous to try to do everything anyway. Option B: Ignore her. She'll stop whining if you just don't pay any attention to her. To ensure that you won't have to listen to her, sign her up for another committee at the school. Option C: Hold her in the center of your heart with kindness. Let her know that no matter what, you are there for her and that you love her. Listen deeply to hear her experience so she knows she is not alone. She is much more than the number of crossed-off items on her daily to-do list. Perhaps suggest constructive ways to reduce some of her burdens.

If you're reading this, it's a pretty good bet that you picked option C. We relate to our friends with compassion and understanding because we've been there too, and we know exquisitely how it feels.

When you're not in a loving space towards yourself, remember this exercise. Hold in your mind the words and thoughts you would offer your friend who comes to you for help. Now switch the lens and imagine that you are offering the same kindness to yourself. If you hear a "BUT, I'm (fill in the blank)," recognize that "BUT" as a signal that you're on to something good for you—and keep going. Don't stop the exercise or listen to the BUT-talk. Feel whatever comes up, such as awkwardness or a feeling that you may not be deserving of this kindness. Feel where it lodges in your body. Notice and send breath there. Then, go back to holding yourself in that same loving light of healing you offered to your friend. We are so good at offering nurturing to others, aren't we? Embracing ourselves with that same nurturing light can truly transform your relationship to yourself, and in turn, will help heal and deepen your relationships with those you love

This embodied exercise will help you look in that mirror and instead of seeing what needs to be improved or corrected, see the vibrant, magnificent woman and mother shining back at you. Sure, there may be some aspects of your life you want to change— but do it from this place of loving who you are, right now. My first yoga teacher waited for a life-threatening diagnosis to reorganize his life. Let us not do that—we can realign our vision of ourselves with purposeful kindness now. We are exquisitely aware that that this body, this family, this life, these moments all are so precious and entirely ours to live right now. And, if life events have catapulted you into a difficult phase, then now is the time to double down on this kindness to yourself. Taking this radical step towards self-compassion is seriously a huge community service effort — by being more generous with ourselves, we give others in our families and communities the "ok" to be kinder and more generous with themselves. Self-care and compassion are contagious in the best possible way.

HEALING YOGA POSE: *Setu Bandhasana.* (Bridge Pose). Lie onto your back and bend your knees. Place your feet on the floor so that your ankles are directly underneath your knees. Separate your feet so that they are hip-width distance apart from each other. Make sure that the outer edge of each foot is parallel to the side of the mat—not heels in, or heels out, but instead, straight. Your heels should be close enough to you that you can gently touch the back of them with your fingertips. On an inhale, press down evenly through your feet and lift your hips off the ground. Interlace your hands underneath you so that you are on the outer edge of your shoulders. Press your forearms directly down into the mat. Let your chest expand upward so that you can breathe fully into your lungs. Engage your butt muscles here to help stabilize the pelvis. Reach your lower back towards the back of your knees. Maintain this posture for at least five breaths. On the fifth breath, exhale and release your hips to the ground, separate your hands so your arms rest alongside you. Breathe smoothly. You can repeat this pose 3-5 times.

BENEFITS: *Increases stamina and energy. Healthfully stimulates your adrenal glands. Strengthens your gluteus muscles and hamstrings. Breaks up tension in the back. Opens chest, increasing circulation and deepening the breath. Invigorating, energy-giving pose.*

BE-KIND-TO-YOUR-MINDSPEAK: I love myself with the same energy that I love my children with. My energy is clear and powerful because I am wholeheartedly embracing this moment.

Figure 18: *Setu Bandhasana* (Bridge Pose)

GET BALANCED: LOVE YOURSELF AS YOU LOVE YOUR NEIGHBOR

GET BALANCED:
Hit the Reset Button

In this age of constant bombardment, the science is clear: if you want your mind and body to last, you've got to prioritize giving them a rest.

Melanie Curtain

A prominent on-line yoga retailer put out a message recently that astonished me. It read as follows: "Do you feel run down amidst the ever-increasing pace of life? … With these yoga asanas, you can bust through your stagnation." I don't know about you, but that suggestion, borne from our culture that encourages The Fantasy of SuperMom, strikes me as the opposite of balance, health, and well-being. Frankly, it completely misses the point to look and listen inwardly, to be present to our selves, and to be real. It misses the point of enjoying motherhood and savoring the time that we have as we raise our families. Resting and recharging is an essential ingredient in any situation, and especially for us moms. "Busting through"— smacks of the idea that you should do it all, be it all, and look unbelievably ageless and tireless while effortlessly singing through the day. And if you aren't doing it this way, the story goes, then you probably aren't doing it right. Well, my friends: Screw that.

When you're tired, rest. When you're frazzled, take a break. Pause. Use the space between thoughts as a mini-break. Deepen your compassion for yourself and for those involved. How do you do that? Below are several embodied practices that you can turn to when you're tired, or even when you feel great and want to keep the momentum of your joy going. The suggestions create the acronym, MINDFUL. You probably won't be surprised to see that none of the offerings is to run around doing more power yoga.

M. Mini-Meditation. Before you get out of bed in the morning, give yourself five minutes to do a quick meditation. This may mean setting the alarm five minutes earlier than when the kids get up. You can use any number of guided meditations on phone apps, free meditations on YouTube, or simply breathe and focus your mind onto the sensations of breath entering and exiting your body. Yes, your mind will wander; that's expected. Gently but firmly bring your thoughts back to a focal point—either your breath, or a mantra such as "peace," or "relax." In study after study, including work at University of California-Davis by MacLean (2010), meditation has been shown to improve our ability to concentrate. It also helps us build the "letting go" muscle. Meditation allows us to literally watch how impermanent thoughts are, which, in turn, helps us let them go.

I. Integrate a mindful yoga practice into your life. Restorative yoga, or any yoga that helps you feel calmer. You may feel too strapped for time for this, but even ten minutes a day will help release the tightness that settles into our muscles when we get stressed. If you find this a difficult routine to establish in your day, then pair your home practice with something else that is non-negotiable, like brushing your teeth. For me, I practice in the morning before the kids get up. That way, it's just part of my day before other responsibilities get in the way. It's part of my "me time." If you don't have a ton of time, agree to at least a 2-minute practice. Set a timer so you can relax into this chunk of time. Check out some of our free practices at www.dawndavis.com, where we have offered mini-yoga practices.

N. Nap. As in, mid-afternoon, 15-20 minutes. I often set aside this time right before I pick the kids up from school. It helps me refuel so I am present to reconnect with them. Let me tell you, we all benefit from my 15-20. I'm less frazzled and that means I'm less likely to overreact. If you still find this difficult to do, remember that the National Sleep Foundation shows that after napping, people report feeling more alert, less stressed, and in a better mood. Think of this mini cat-nap as a valuable investment in the quality of the rest of your day.

D. Deep breaths. Inhale deeply. Exhale slowly. Among other things, deep breathing activates the vagus nerve, which helps switch the nervous system from fight/flight/freeze to a more relaxed awareness. The deeper breathing, especially if you include a few seconds of holding the breath in after you inhale, induces the "relaxation response" (Benson, 1999). Additionally, deep breathing boosts our immune system and releases anti-stress enzymes. Do it anytime, but if it happens to be a circus at your house, do it a lot. You don't have to sound like Darth Vader when you deep breathe, just simple, but conscious full breathing will work wonders.

F. Friend. Treat yourself like you would a good friend. If a friend came to you depleted, how would you respond? Tap into the mindset of warmth and nurturance you'd offer her. Now, pretend for the moment that you are that friend. It'll probably feel strange at first to do this exercise, but stick with it. Dare to give yourself that same energy of kindness you share with those you love. What does "your friend" (hint: that's you) need right now? Perhaps it's a walk in the fresh air, mindfully eating something nourishing, or doing something creative like writing or painting or dancing. Practicing kindness towards yourself may be the most powerful posture of all.

U. Unselfish acts of charity. There is substantial evidence, including work by Konrath (2011), that altruistic behaviors are linked to better health outcomes. You may feel like, wait a minute, I'm doing unselfish acts all day long with my kids! But it could be argued that we benefit directly from giving to our own children. The type of giving that this suggestion refers to is donating time or money to those you may not know, except in the context of the charitable work. Doing so draws us closer to the truth that all humans and animals are interconnected through our vulnerabilities.

L. Laughter. Laughing releases good-feeling hormones, such as dopamine, endorphins and nitric oxide. These are the same hormones that not only combat aging, but also help us feel less stressed. Maybe you can replay in your mind one of the funny things your child did, check out the latest comedian on the internet, or watch something on Netflix that is hilarious. Whatever gets you cracking up!

I'd like you to think of this list the way you think about shopping. You don't go into the store and grab everything off the shelves. Take what you need, as much as you need, at exactly the time you need it.

HEALING YOGA POSE: *Vipariti Karani.* (Restorative Legs Up the Wall Pose). In this version of Vipariti Karani, use the wall to deepen the restorative component of this pose. Grab a pillow and at least one blanket. If you have a yoga strap, please bring it to the wall with you. Fold up one blanket so it's about two to three inches thick. Sit on the floor next to a wall. Put the side of your left hip up against the wall and then pivot so you are lying on your back, butt close to the wall and back of your legs leaning against the wall. You may need to scooch your butt closer to the wall to get there. Then lift your hips up so you can put the folded blanket under your hips. Place the pillow under your neck and head so your neck is supported. Rest your arms alongside you, palms up to the ceiling. You can breathe in this posture for five minutes or longer. If you choose to stay here longer, make a loop with a yoga strap and place the looped strap loosely above your knees to hold your legs together. This way, your legs can relax into the pose but you don't have to hold them up (the strap and the wall are doing that work for you). B.K.S. Iyengar has dubbed this pose "the fountain of youth", so why not rest in it as long as possible?!

BENEFITS: *Soothes the nervous system. Improves circulation and decreases the pressure in varicose veins. Increases energy flow to the brain, reduces pooling of lymph in the feet. Deeply relaxing.*

BE-KIND-TO-YOUR-MINDSPEAK: I rest when I am tired. I eat when I am hungry. I breathe deeply through my day, inviting in my mindfulness and compassion. I love my life.

Figure 19: *Vipariti Karani* (Restorative Legs Up the Wall Pose)

GET BALANCED:
The 3 D's: Death, Divorce, Diagnosis

We can't arrange peace or lasting improvement for the people we love most in the world. They have to find their own ways, their own answers…on their hero's journey."

Anne LaMott

In the span of five weeks, a friend was diagnosed with cancer, another separated from her husband of 15 years, and another lost her father to a massive heart attack. Like any of you would, if I could've taken away their pain, wrapped it up in a big ball and tossed it away, I would've done so in an instant. Instead, casseroles were made, cards were written, and hugs were given. Yet, a preoccupation lingered that exerted a dampening and distracting effect on the way I parented. I found that while my children were trying to get my attention, I was thinking about what was going on in these friends' lives. My energy was splintered in multiple directions, and that contributed to a palpable feeling of depletion. My mothering, which requires a fair amount of effort on a good day, became freighted.

Perhaps you, too, have noticed the uncomfortable truth—as we get older, letting go and loss become more prevelant in our lives. In the extreme, these tend to come in the form of one the three Ds: Death, Divorce, or Diagnosis. Often, when we personally experience a loss, we can manage. When people we love suffer, the natural wish to help them is strong. But when helping those outside of our family interferes with our primary job (taking care of ourselves and our family), then it's time to pause.

Most of us care so much that we put our own needs at the bottom of the list when someone we love is hurting. Maybe we do this because it feels selfish to self-care, especially when the backdrop is a loved one's pain. We can feel guilty that we are enjoying our lives when those we love are suffering. What I've found is initially counter-intuitive but if you can get past the paradox, there is something very valuable in this—we can care more by caring a little less.

To take care of ourselves under normal circumstances requires self-respect; to do so when others we love are hurting takes courage. It doesn't mean not caring— but it does mean being mindful to how much energy we are spending in taking care of others that are not our primary charge. To get there, we must get into a head-space where we examine both the quantity and quality of our own thoughts. First—the quantity of thoughts. This is simultaneously simple and difficult to accomplish. How much time are you spending thinking about their situation? Sometimes it feels like we can't help it, we keep thinking about our loved one's concerns, spending a lot of energy doing so. I've noticed that if I'm not paying attention, I'll go over the painful situation again and again in a kind of loop. This is the sand trap in the golf course of over-caring for others. It's really important to notice if your mind has been consumed by such looping and redirect your attention to thoughts that are less weighted. Though our hearts are definitely in the right place, spending our energy in this way may not be the most effective way to offer help.

In addition, the quality of what we are thinking matters. Have you ever noticed that even though you may not personally be going through a traumatic experience, that doesn't mean that you aren't experiencing fear, worry, or anger. Notice and allow these feelings. Don't resist the feelings— as you probably know, resisting emotions actually makes them stronger. Instead, allow the feelings to come up, wash over you, and then move through you. As you do this, is it possible to be attentive and compassion towards yourself? This "getting out of the way" in the context of kindness helps the feelings run their course without creating blocks of stagnant energy within you.

I've also found it useful to bear in mind Marianne Williamson's idea that our loved one's suffering didn't show up empty-handed; it came with spiritual gifts to help get them through the darkness. Remember that we are not responsible for their decisions or their journey; however, we can help create a context for their recovery. Much like when your child skins their knee; our job is to set the stage of healing through using antibiotic creams and bandaids. The healing will take place of its own natural timing and process. We can be the midwives of their experience, helping and coaching and encouraging, but we can't actually do the labor for them.

HEALING YOGA POSE: *Prasarita Padottanasana C.* (Standing Wide-Legged Forward Fold Pose). Stand, facing one side of the room, with your feet separated approximately 3-4 feet away from each other. Turn your toes in towards each other slightly, heels slightly further out. Interlace your fingers behind your back. Inhale and reach your heart up towards the ceiling. This will pull you into a slight backbend. Engage your core. As you exhale, bend your knees slightly, lean forward, hinging at your hips. Your head will drop towards the floor. Allow your interlaced hands and arms to reach towards the ceiling, or even out in front of you. Straighten your knees without locking them. Maintain engagement of your core, thighs, and then engage your perineum (like a kegel). Continue to gently reach the crown of your head towards the floor. Lean forward into the pose, letting your body weight move towards the balls of your feet. Breathe here for 10 breaths. Release your hands to your hips, bend your knees, and with your core engaged, come up to standing with an elongated spine.

BENEFITS: *Anti-stress, anti-anxiety pose. Also stretches hamstrings, calves and opens shoulder joints. Relaxes your mind into a calmer state.*

BE-KIND-TO-YOUR-MINDSPEAK: The better care I take of myself, the better able I'll be to care for my loved ones. I love my life, and I give wholeheartedly to others because I give wholeheartedly to myself.

Figure 20: *Prasarita Padottanasana C* (Standing Wide-Legged Forward Fold Pose)

THE KINDNESS CREW

This section goes directly to the heart of the matter—being kinder to ourselves. It not only makes us feel great, but it increases our energy, allows us to be more fully present with our kids, and to feel more centered. In addition, by being kinder to ourselves, we model this important self-treatment for our kids.

THE KINDNESS CREW:
Savor It, Don't Save It!

The big miracles we're waiting on are happening right in front of us, at every moment, with every breath. Open your eyes and your heart and you'll begin to see them.

Oprah Winfrey

On her 9th birthday, we gave our daughter "ballet sneakers." Leading up to receiving this gift, she talked about these special shoes at every opportunity, danced around the house as if she was already in them, and begged my husband and me to buy them for her. Moments after she opened the box, she slipped these pinkalicious sneaker shoes onto her hungry feet, an extra spring in her already-bouncy step. "I love them!!" she cooed as she twirled around the house in these fantastic, over-priced, long-awaited shoes.

So, it was with some surprise when I didn't see the shoes again for days. And then a week or so went by. And then another and another week. When I asked her about them, she replied "I LOVE them! I'm just saving them."

The reality about kids: they grow. And grow and grow. So, when those precious shoes came out again a couple months later, they were tight. And that was just the beginning. Eventually too tight to wear. She had protected her shoes from getting dirty, but she herself hadn't had the experience of enjoying them.

I can see myself in this save it attitude. As parents, we often save it for later or, cling a little too tightly. I'm not talking about delayed-gratification, or even the push towards a goal—I'm talking about the hard-won experience of getting exactly what you've worked for, but *instead of savoring it*, we "*save*" it. Like when we save the good china for "special" occasions, rather than using it more frequently. Or perhaps more importantly, when we hold back on putting ourselves 100% into the moment, the conversation, the yoga pose, the whatever, because we are "saving" our energy.

Wouldn't it be something: if we could relax in the moment with the already-present joys, savoring the juice out of them, and trusting that the next moment will be different, but possibly equally satisfying? After all, we know life is temporary. Maybe it's precisely because we are aware that life is impermanent that we find it difficult to relax into each moment. Ironic, of course, because armed with the knowledge that this moment won't last, we might instead be able to enjoy what each moment. But, it doesn't always work this way.

As in the case of the shoes, we often resist what is good in our lives. We unintentionally fight relaxing into the present. How can we, as Eckert Tolle encourages us, to "say 'yes' to the present moment. Surrender to what is. Say 'yes' to life—and see how life starts suddenly to start working for you rather than against you"? How is that possible when there is so much internal chatter that keeps us away from really embracing the joys that are already here?

Attempting to make inroads to relaxing more with what is present, I turned to the teachings of Jon Kabat Zinn, the founder of the Mind Based Stress Reduction Clinic. Though he is talking about thinking in general, it can be effectively applied to this situation of robbing our joy by too much internal resistance. Specifically, he suggests that we notice the inner chatter and then simply witness the thoughts float by. The way you might feel if you were sitting on the banks of a river and watching water. You don't have to get caught up in the currents of that river (your thoughts). You can sit on the grassy banks and watch the thoughts course by, consciously bringing your mind's attention back to your breath, and back to the present moment. You can engage in this witnessing your thoughts-business in the midst of the mind chatter as you go through your day. However, if you do a couple minutes of meditation in the morning, you'll powerfully strengthen your capacity to witness your own thoughts float by when you're in the heat of the moment later in the day. By doing this, we make even greater strides to receiving the joys that are present in our lives.

Staying connected to a joyful vibe is one of the kindest things we can do for ourselves. It'll increase our energy and likely contribute to an overall good feeling in the house. Notice when the connection to joy gets derailed by worry or overthinking—and then step out of the current of thoughts and onto the riverbanks to witness them float by. In this way, we can come back to the experience the joys, lightness, and vibrancy of as many moments as possible.

HEALING YOGA POSE: Five-minute meditation. Set your timer on your phone or device for five minutes (if you only have two minutes, do this for two then—or even one minute is better than no minute). Sit comfortably, or even lie down. Close your eyes and just take notice of your breath. Is it shallow? Is it deep? Don't judge it, just notice it and then purposefully breathe in through your nose, feeling your abdomen expand to take in the breath. Feel how the breath takes up space inside your body. Notice how the presence of the breath softens the internal organs, creating a spacious expansion internally. I love to say to myself, "smooth, slow, steady" as I inhale, suggesting that the breath represent those qualities (and the mind quickly follows suit). Next, exhale through your nose, noticing how the abdomen and chest deflate as the breath leaves your body. On the exhale, I say "smooth, slow, steady", again a conditioner for the mind. Notice the thoughts floating by, and then kindly bring them back to focus on your breath. You might have to bring your attention back to your breath 100 times during the five minutes. The most important moment, as Sharon Saltzberg reminds us, is when we notice we're "gone," and bring ourselves back to breath.

BENEFITS: *Calms the mind chatter. Improves focus, concentration, and memory. Creates a feeling of internal peace, soothes and calms the nervous system.*

BE-KIND-TO-YOUR-MINDSPEAK: I drop in and savor this moment. I say YES to my life. I relax and open to the joys of my life.

Figure 21: *Seated Meditation Practice*

KINDNESS FIRST:
The Trap of the Get-It-Done Attitude

Don't postpone joy until you have learned all your lessons. Joy is your lesson.

Allan Cohen

I personally have hated folding laundry. It feels like a task made for Sisyphys—the Greek God who pushed the boulder up the mountainside, only to have it fall back on him time and again. He never reached the top. For years, I have felt this way about the clean clothes. But, catching myself saying, "can't wait till these baskets are folded, then I can relax" was a moment of awakening for me.

I realized I was postponing my joy in this small way, which led me to examine where else in my life I was postponing my joy. I saw little bits of postponement all over my life. So, I took the task in front of me—the dreaded laundry—and overrode my default intention (get it done and quick) with the conscious intention to feel joy while I folded laundry. At first, my mind bucked—"I'm not going to pretend I like this, when I actually hate the monotony of it!" I heard this mini-rant and then, almost like an experiment, I settled back into my conscious intention: what would it feel like if I sincerely intended to feel joy while I undertook this task of laundry? Keeping it real, I didn't start clicking my heels in exuberance, or whistling like Snow White with the seven dwarfs, but something in me shifted.

The task was the same, yet I had changed. I could actually see the clothes in front of me, maybe for the first time in a long time. I held onto a pink-striped shirt that now belonged to my youngest child, which once belonged to my middle child, and before that belonged to my oldest one. The clothes became a reminder not to take this moment for granted, because in a very short time, each of them will have outgrown all these clothes and eventually, each of them will have grown up and out of our family home. There is nothing quite as powerful as the larger perspective of the passing of time that brings home the message—be present in this moment, right here.

There always will be more laundry to fold (unless you're reading this naked, you're actually creating laundry right now). There always will be someone else to email, another carpool to run, another lunch to make. And for many, it feels like there always will be another goal to attain, another status to achieve, and another milestone to put in the rearview mirror.

The thinking goes, once I complete my to-do list, or once I/they feel better, or we reach that financial goal, or go on vacation, or get through the holidays, then I can feel the relief, joy, and relaxation I crave. It's as if we have a formula that says only after XYZ happens, then can we let ourselves chill. I wonder how often we unintentionally quashed our enthusiasm and passion because we were hyper-focused on getting-it-done and moving on to the next thing?

In my humble thinking, the quintessential secret to lasting enthusiasm and relaxation is to bring this truth into each situation. In reality, there will never be a day like the one you are living, never be a time like the one you are in now. Fully embodying that truth will let us enjoy our children's tender years, recognizing the challenges and the beauty in each moment, but honoring the wish to be present more than the wish to have it all done.

So, I believe we have choices—especially when it comes to our thoughts. Perhaps the idea of having two minds—similar to what Michael Singer says—is useful here. For our purposes, one mind is wise and knowing, the Soul Mind. The other mind is the Immature Mind and has a lower vibration. The belief that "we must wait till it's completed in order to feel joy" is simply a trick produced by the Immature Mind. We can't blame it, after all it was forged during our childhood when we believed that once we grew up, we'd have freedom; once we completed school, we could relax; once we earned money, we'd feel accomplished; once we fell in love, we'd belong and feel cherished; once we had children, we'd have meaningfully contributed; once we have XYZ, we could really start living. The Immature Mind thrives on keeping us one step away from our joy because that is all it knew. It doesn't mean to steal your life away, but it just doesn't know how else to exist. We can choose to let the Immature Mind run the show. Or we can allow recognize that the Immature Mind will always be a piece of the puzzle, but it doesn't have to steal the show.

We can let the Immature Mind drop into the background and amp up the volume of the Soul Mind.

The Soul Mind is your witness. It is imbued with Supreme essence and is steeped in some serious wisdom. It is that part of you that says, "Be Still and Know." By listening more attentively to the Soul Mind, we are positioned to accomplish the simple and not-so-simple work of our lives with greater moments of awareness and awe, as well as passion and relaxed joy. And these moments, when culled together, deepen our purpose, vibrancy and love, not only for ourselves but for our families and for this precious world.

The way to disarm the Immature Mind is to first recognize it when it shows up. Next, set an intention from your Soul Mind, the more eternal aspect of your being. It could be the intention to drink in the moments with your children, to prepare activities for them that will make memories for all of you, or even to be less stressed so you can enjoy the mundane stuff of making lunches, folding laundry, and cleaning house. By seeking joy in the everyday, we celebrate the simplicity of being alive together. We honor the mundane because, when you think about it, the majority of our lives are spent knee-deep in the simple and the mundane. Let today be the day that you release any internal resistance that prevents you from surrendering into the present moment.

HEALING YOGA POSE: *Upavistha Konasana.* (Wide-legged Seated Forward Fold Pose, with/without Twist). Place a blanket underneath your sitting bones and sit upright with a tall spine, legs in front of you. Bend your right knee and open your right leg out wide to the right. Then, repeat with the left leg so that both legs are separated, knee caps pointing to the ceiling and toes flexed back towards knees. You're in a seated straddle position, sitting bones pressing into the floor. Draw your outer thighs towards the floor and lengthen both legs away from each other. Now place your hands in front of you. Slowly walk them further away from your torso. Hinge at your hips so that your torso is moving closer towards the floor but be mindful to maintain a long spine. Do you feel a stretch through your groins and your hamstrings? Use your exhales to draw you closer towards the floor and more gently into the pose. Take 10 breath here. To deepen the pose, use a strap or your right hand to take hold of your right big toe. Drop your right elbow on top of or inside of your right knee. Use your left arm above you to further extend the pose by wrapping your bicep past your left ear. Reach your left fingers towards your right toes. Actively push through your left leg as your twist your left ribs up towards the ceiling. Take five to eight breaths here and then come back to a neutral seated position. Repeat on the left side.

BENEFITS: *Releases tension in the inner groins, loosens up hamstrings and hip joints. Relaxes the mind and increases breathing capacity. Gently stimulates the abdominal organs. If you choose the variation with the twist, you will also be lengthening the muscles of the back, specifically the Quadratus Lumborum (the QL).*

BE-KIND-TO-YOUR-MINDSPEAK: Today I amplify the volume of my Soul Mind. I set my intention to enjoy each precious moment with my loved ones and to stay connected to broader joy and vibrant love. I release resistance to the present and step into this moment. I am here and happy to receive.

Figure 22: *Upavistha Konasana* (Wide-legged Seated Forward Fold Pose, with/without Twist)

THE KINDNESS CREW:
A Self Critic is Born

When we are in the trance of unworthiness, we're not aware of how much our body, emotions, and thoughts have locked into a sense of falling short and the fear that we're going to fail. It makes it difficult to be intimate, spontaneous and real with others, because we have the sense that, even if they don't already know, they will find out how flawed we really are. It makes it hard to take risks because we're afraid we're going to fall short. We can never really relax. Right in the heart of the trance, there is a need to do something to be better, to avoid the failure lurking right around the corner.

Tara Brach

Perhaps you've noticed that we live in a culture that sets ridiculous expectations for women and mothers. Between the gap of that expectation and the reality of being human, runs a river of inadequacy. That river brings to life the self-critic. Its appearance can start early, go deep, and then show up in a myriad of ways as we progress through our lives.

The new and shiny version of ourselves, we were taught to believe, comes after tearing the house down. Yet, some of our greatest thinkers remind us that we can't condemn ourselves into sustained change. Even Einstein says that we can't solve a problem with the same level of consciousness that created the problem. Building on a deficit doesn't work.

Sometimes the self-condemnation is subtle, but wow, is it persistent. We might criticize ourselves for not having the patience of a saint, the perfect kids, a larger bank account, or the body that we had 20 years ago. It may be little comments that are periodically undermining, or it may be an internal rant that is consistently demoralizing. It may not only be the presence of negative internal comments about ourselves, but also the lack of acknowledging our own accomplishments that creates the conditions for the self-critic to emerge. All I know is that when the self-critic enters a room, love and kindness walk out the door.

The kicker is that when we put ourselves down a lot, it's hard to see those we are closest to for who they are. Like emotional pink-eye, self-criticism encrusts our eyes with itchy, uncomfortable gunk, obscuring the beauty of not only ourselves, but of those we love. Have you ever noticed that the more we criticize ourselves, the easier it is to criticize those around us?

Anyway, even knowing that the self-critic isn't really our best friend, and that the self-critic doesn't actually make our lives happier doesn't mean that we can easily get rid of it. I've tried to get the self-critic to quit her day job (and her middle-of-the-night-job, too), and only found that she had taken up fairly permanent residence in my mind. As Tara Brach reminds us, it's akin to being in a trance. Its tenacity is not personal, it's not some idiosyncratic failing of ours. It's simply how the brain is wired. Neuroscience teaches us that the more we repeat certain thoughts— be they uplifting, or off-putting—the deeper the neural groove gets. The thoughts literally create a pathway in the brain that is the easiest road to travel on. The self-critic emits is foul vibes on auto-pilot simply because it has done this time and time again. The good news is that no matter how bad the self-critic may be right now, we can use this same technique of repeating loving thoughts towards ourselves to create new roads that are far more supportive and happy.

But, in order to make sustained change in the thinking department and move towards a deeper self-love, it's essential to explore why we thought listening to the self-critic was a good idea in the first place. I don't know about you, but somewhere along the line, I bought into the belief that putting myself down would make me better at (fill in the blank). Have you ever noticed this in yourself? Perhaps it's because we believe it will motivate us. And it can—in the short run. You want to lose some weight? Beat yourself into submission, deprive yourself, and then you might get on the treadmill. For a few days or even a couple of weeks. But, because the motivation is coming from a place of anxiety and anger, it's no wonder it's next to impossible to sustain. You want to be a better parent? Fear can get a fire under you and you might even implement some parenting strategies that seem to work in the short-run. But the transformation is short-lived. It's akin to building a beautiful home without laying a solid foundation. The house initially looks good, but in no time at all, it begins to crumble because the base of the home was not sturdy. A solid foundation here includes loving kindness towards ourselves, not fear-based criticism. Donna Farhi as well as Pema Chodron beautifully note that whenever we engage in self-improvement, we run the risk of abusing ourselves. If we don't engage in self-improvement with a healthy dose of kindness and compassion, the change we seek will not last, and we'll probably feel like crap in the meantime.

Okay, so we know the self-critic was created because we were trying to improve something in our lives and we are also aware that habitual thought patterns that keep the self-critic in place are simply how the brain is wired. So, how do we release the self-critic so that we can make improvements in our lives from a place of loving kindness, laying down healthy and positive neural pathways?

I've tried to get rid of the self-critic by beating myself up for having the self-critic in the first place, and I've tried to get rid of the self-critic by doubling down on my fear and efforts to change, believing that once I achieved the goal, the self-critic would leave. Um. These attempts didn't work. The self-critic stuck around. It simply shifted gears to something else — and prevented me from enjoying the accomplishments I had created.

It was only when I began to connect to the vulnerability in my self-critic that she began to simmer down some. The self-critic is trying to help us, though she is doing it in a fairly brutal way. Her rants became quiet when I told myself that I love that part of myself that is criticizing me. Strange as it may initially sound, I've found it a powerful moment of transformation when I sent that self-critic my love. Not only did it disarm the self-critic (after all, she thrives on our resistance and push back), but it puts us back in charge of our own minds. We are conveying, loudly and clearly, that every aspect of ourselves is encompassed by our kind and loving embrace. No part of us is left out in the cold, trying to attention-grab. Not even the self-critic can hide from the light of our love. Loving the voice of the self-critic spells freedom.

Holding every part of ourselves—the amazing as well as the unruly and mean parts—with tenderness is not only soothing, it is in fact, curative. We don't have to punish ourselves to become our best self. We can model for our children that self-improvement doesn't have to harsh or disrespectful. Love all of you. How amazing would it be if our children approached their own self-growth from a place of cherishing who they are? Let today be the day that you decide that you are growing into the woman and mother you want to be, with love woven into every fiber of your dreams, your life, and even woven into the voice of your self-critic.

HEALING YOGA POSE: *Adho Muka Svasana.* (Downward Dog Pose). Start in a tabletop position, on all fours, with knees and hands pressing into the floor. Your knees are hip-width distance apart and your hands are shoulder-width distance apart. Spine is in neutral here, and you'll draw your abdomen into your spine. As you inhale, turn your toes under your feet, and raise your hips. During the transition from tabletop to Downward Dog, engage your thigh muscles as well as your abdominal muscles. Once your hips are elevated, extend your spine long, and drop your head so that your neck muscles can soften and relax. Your body is now in an inverted-V shape. Spin your triceps towards your outer heels. Can you lift your sitting bones any higher here? If you feel rounding in your lower back, then bend both knees. Close your eyes or gaze softly at one point in between your feet. Take 5-10 relaxed and easy breaths.

BENEFITS: *Lengthens spinal column to relieve tension in the back. Extends the back of the body, including hamstrings and calves. Strengthens upper body muscles, especially triceps and shoulders. Improves breathing. Calms the mind.*

BE-KIND-TO-YOUR-MINDSPEAK: I cherish myself exactly as I am, with all my flaws and all my fabulousness. I am complete in this moment. Today, I relax by being loving and kind to me.

Figure 23: *Adho Muka Svasana (Downward Dog Pose)*

THE KINDNESS CREW:
Friendliness Towards Ourselves & Chocolate

Be careful how you are talking to yourself because you are listening.

Lisa M. Hayes

On a recent rainy afternoon, my daughter and I baked a pan of brownies. When those sumptuous morsels came out of the oven, the intoxicating smell of warm chocolate filled the kitchen. I had a sliver, just a "little bit more." But it wasn't quite enough, and I needed another sliver. The wish for the third sliver was joined by a little anger at myself for wanting more. The real kicker is that frustration at myself prevented me from enjoying the subsequent brownie. As I didn't enjoy it in the first place, I went in for another and still unsatisfying slice.

At that moment, I wondered—how can I find the sweetness here? Could it be found by treating myself with such disapproval and disrespect? Probably not. In fact, if a friend stopped by, would I judge her for wanting more brownies? Not a chance. I'd generously offer her the delectable confections and feel gratitude that she was enjoying our creation. It would be unimaginable to not be gracious and generous to a friend in this way. Returning my thoughts to myself, I realized that if I don't relax enough, I won't be able to receive the sweetness of this moment, these brownies, these children. It's all intimately connected—the way we treat ourselves in the private little moments directly relates to how we treat ourselves in the important more marked moments.

So, I'm a chocoholic apparently. I moved toward the pan again, this time through the eyes of love that I'd share with a good friend. Eyes of receptivity. Eyes of gentleness and genuine kindness. Not eyes that criticize and berate. As if I was my own bestie, I cut myself a good-sized square, right from the center of the pan (my favorite brownies live there). I put this chocolate glowing thing on a plate and poured myself a glass of milk. I got a napkin and sat down at the island counter next to my daughter.

And I lovingly ate and tasted and enjoyed every fabulous crumb.

By treating myself as I would a good friend, rather than some animal that needs to be controlled for fear of going wild, I felt satisfied. I opened up to the sweetness in that moment and my connection with my daughter deepened as I was able to see her clearly, instead of through the filter of my negative self-chatter about my thing for sweets. This simple experience reminded me that life offers us many opportunities like this.

What if every situation in our lives—from the mundane to the exquisite—were approached through the loving eyes that we beam to our loved ones? For example, when we are gripped by frustration about a situation, rather than criticize ourselves, offer compassion to ourselves in the same way we would offer to a friend who struggles with a self-doubt or two. What if you were to juice the joy out of your life, the way you would wish that your child savors the joys of hers? That means surrendering to the pleasurable moments without reservations, apologies, or guilt. Tall order, but worth the inquiry.

How do we even know when we're not seeing ourselves through the eyes of the beloved? Sometimes it's clear as day, but other times, it's more subtle. For me, the more subtle ways I am aware that I'm not seeing myself through the eyes of the beloved is that I'll feel tension around my eyes, especially my temples on the sides of my face. Sometimes I'll notice that I've been clenching my teeth. These are the body's wisdom signals that it is time to pause and shift the way I'm relating to myself.

Physical messages from our body are valuable clues pointing to whether we are off center. Tara Brach calls it "embodied awareness" and believes it holds the keys to our happiness. Today, what if you were to approach yourself tenderly, with trust, and an undeniable friendliness. Shifting your vision may feel awkward at first, but anything new can feel awkward at first. What would happen if you allowed awkwardness to be a part of the experience and recognize its appearance as an indication that you're growing here? Each time the negative self-chatter shows up in your own psyche, open your heart to yourself as you would a good friend who you would want to know how much you cherish her. Loving ourselves in this way will open and transform us into the brilliance of who we really are.

HEALING YOGA POSE: *Virabhadrasana II.* (Warrior II Pose). Similar to Warrior I, come into a lunge with your right foot forward and your left leg extended behind you. However, for Warrior II, you'll drop your left foot to the floor so that it is essentially parallel to the back of your mat. Bring yourself up to standing and bend into your right knee, so it is over your right ankle. Be mindful that the knee doesn't go past your ankle (if it is, just walk your right foot up until the ankle and knee are lined up). Extend both arms away from you, so shoulders, elbows and wrists are all in one line. Palms face down as your arms energetically stretch away from your torso. Your chest is open, and your hips are open to the side of your mat. Shoulders are squared above your hips. Gaze over your extended front hand. Plug your big toe mounds into the earth and then slightly lift your toes off the mat, hovering in padabandha. Breathe for 8-10 deep breaths. Can you feel an expansiveness in your chest here? Repeat with your left foot forward.

BENEFITS: *Strengths thigh and hamstring of front leg. Opens the hip flexors and inner thigh of the back leg. Builds strength in upper back, biceps and triceps. Strengths neck muscles. Improves concentration. A solidly grounding pose.*

BE-KIND-TO-YOUR-MINDSPEAK: I look at myself through the eyes of love. I am my own best friend, honoring and accepting myself and my desires. I love who I am.

Figure 24: *Virabhadrasana II (Warrior II Pose)*

THE KINDNESS CREW: FRIENDLINESS TOWARDS OURSELVES & CHOCOLATE

THE KINDNESS CREW:
What They Think of You

Virtually all of our problems are either caused or compounded by our obsessive need for acceptance and approval from other people…To the degree that I live my life in an effort to please others, I chip away at myself.

Terry Cole-Whittaker

When it's all said and done, it won't matter what they think of you. And often, it's not even what they think of you; it's what *you think* they think of you. Have you ever noticed that anticipating what others think of us, and then shaping our behavior to please them, pulls us away from our center and drains our battery? The battery I'm talking about is your own powerful guidance system, your own vitality, your own enthusiasm.

For years, I caused myself a good deal of pain by anticipating what my friends, family members, and even acquaintances would think or want from me. It wasn't that I explicitly wanted anyone's approval per se, but that I wanted to be pleasing and helpful—sometimes so much so that I was willing to relinquish my own wishes in the process. Sometimes my feelers were subtle, sometimes explicit, but they were there, humming along like cheesy music in the background of my life. I'd worry that "they" would be mad if I didn't organize the bake sale, or that they would think less of me if I allowed my daughter drop out of soccer. I'd get caught up in what they would think if my children weren't particularly friendly, and sometimes I'd even worry that they'd be threatened by my kid's successes. My concern about how others saw me was squeezing my size 10 soul into a tight 00. I was strangling my own internal power source with my very own hands.

Truth is, impression management is not going to give me, you, or anyone, the love and satisfaction we all crave. Sadly, it encourages us to squander our energy on something that can never offer us real peace. As Terry Cole-Whittaker emphasizes in *What You Think of Me is None of My Business*, we give away our power when we let others direct where our energy goes. So, instead of creating the life we truly desire, we wind up feeling resentful and depleted. By focusing outward in this way, we unintentionally manipulate who we really are, essentially devaluing our true nature.

The pattern of shaping ourselves to satisfy others' expectations of us is particularly difficult to break because it is everywhere in our culture and it reinforces itself. Over decades, our minds have been trained to get feedback from the outside world to see if we're "doing it right." So, don't be surprised if at first it feels as dangerous as driving at night without the headlights on. Remember that the more you get the feel of your own internal guidance system, the more you'll trust your own wisdom and vision. Then you can stay your course without giving into the whimsy of a pushy neighbor or even the pressure of a well-meaning relative.

How do we harness the power in our own internal guidance system? We have to look at why we alter our own vision to accommodate and fit into the expectation of others around us. For many of us, we do this because when we don't we feel awkward. And that awkwardness is perceived as a sign that we should backtrack to make the other person feel more comfortable (which, in turn, would dissipate that awkward feeling and we'd ultimately feel more comfortable, too). I was so guilty of this and there are times when I still struggle with it.

For instance, for several months, I convinced my daughter, who didn't want to have a playdate with a neighbor's child, to have playdate after playdate with her. I cringe just thinking about it. I pushed my daughter to keep playing because it was clear my neighbor's daughter liked mine and I didn't want to offend my neighbor. I disguised my need to please. I told myself I was teaching my daughter to "roll with it", to be flexible, to have grit. Truth is, I was really teaching my daughter to ignore her true feelings, her own intuition and her own sense of who she liked and didn't like. My daughter's voice and power were getting drowned out by my need to not make the situation awkward.

The light went on in my head one afternoon. My daughter was walking back from the neighbor's house and I could see almost a blanket of resignation draped over her shoulders. I backtracked. I told my daughter that I heard and understood her feelings. Somehow, just reinforcing the notion that she was entitled to her feelings helped her relax (and me, too). We talked about the importance of being kind to others when letting them know that your opinion diverged from theirs. This is the slippery slope because we don't want to hurt someone else's feelings, yet we need to stay true to our own sense of self. This level of sincerity is harder to cultivate than just doing what the neighbor wants. It involves seeing the situation through the other person's perspective, and still, not abandoning your own perspective in the process. So, the next time the neighbor texted for a playdate, I wrote back that it wasn't the right fit right now and that we'd reach out when it was. This may (or may not) have upset my neighbor, but I did something far more important for my own daughter and in doing so, she experienced the unique empowerment that comes from honoring her integrity. We both healed a little that day, merging truth with kindness.

The only way we got to the place of deeper integrity was by working with the feeling of awkwardness. Remember that on this journey, feeling awkward often signals that you're moving in a new and important direction of health. It doesn't mean you should stop and turn around. Rather, look at the feeling of awkwardness in the same way you might when you're physically conditioning your body. It's uncomfortable at times. But, we keep going because we know it is in service of something stronger and healthier. Don't let the wish to avoid awkward feelings pull you off course.

How to stay grounded so that awkwardness doesn't derail you? The next time your wish diverges from another's wishes, engage in a practice that will help you stabilize and root your energy. The meditation that follows is intended to be just that. It'll help you stay centered in the face of other's contrasting wishes, and by doing so, you'll fine-tune your own inner compass. The beauty of this is that you will begin to notice when aspects of any situation are out of alignment with your center. This, in turn, shifts the focus from what others think of you and instead, allows you to stay sensitive to your inner guidance.

Standing confidently in our authentic power as women and as mama bears isn't easy. It means we step into uncomfortable feelings as we honor our deeper wishes. In this way, we model for our children this important life-long skill. It's important to be considerate of others' feelings, but we needn't be overly concerned such that we dismiss our own wisdom. Once we really accept who we are, we are able to find compromises when needed, or at other times, to have the confidence to say "no thanks" and move on. By doing this, we encourage our own children to wade in the warm waters of self-respect, rather than pushing them into the rough seas of pleasing others. As Dr. Michael Beckwith says, we are teaching them to have the courage of their convictions, even if others disagree with them. This is surely protective for them now and as they mature into adulthood.

HEALING YOGA POSE: *Spinal Kriya.* (Visualization Meditation for Increasing Energy). Inhale deeply and hold that breath for three to four counts. Release your breath very slowly, taking twice as long to exhale as you did on inhale (e.g., eight counts on exhale). On your next inhale, picture a white-golden ball of healing light being pulled from the sky, through the crown of your head, and down into your spine. On your exhale, imagine the white golden light filling every cell of your body with protection, healing, and guidance. This sacred nurturing light is within each of us. Employing this technique allows us to consciously connect to this source.

To amplify the effects of this grounding technique, you can include another specific pranayama technique, *Viloma Pranayama.* Take a deep breath in, and then exhale completely. Next, inhale one-third of your breath into your lower abdomen. Pause. Inhale another third of your breath into your middle abdomen. Pause. Now, inhale the final third of your breath into your upper chest. Pause. Exhale a third of your breath from your upper chest, pause. Exhale a third of your breath from your middle abdomen, pause. Exhale the remaining breath from your lower abdomen. Inhale and exhale normally. Repeat two to three more times. Release with an extended exhale.

BENEFITS: *Calm and soothes the nervous system. Promotes clarity of thinking and relaxation. Increases energy and sense of protection and divine guidance.*

BE-KIND-TO-YOUR-MINDSPEAK: I get out of my own way to receive the love that is within me now. My good boundaries are infused with genuineness, truth, and kindness. I have everything I need within my own being right now. I am safe.

Figure 25: *Visualization Meditation*

THE KINDNESS CREW:
Lessons Cinderella Taught Me

Start where you are. Use what you have. Do what you can.

Arthur Ashe

Towards the end of the (2015) *Cinderella* film, Cinderella asks the prince, "Can you take me as I am?" A good and interesting question. She is asking this question because, as you might remember, she is a simple girl with no royal blood, and he is the prince. But perhaps a more valuable question to ask is, can we take ourselves as we are—as the mothers that we are, as the spouses that we are, as the friends that we are, and so on? In other words, can you accept the person that you actually are right now, regardless of whether someone else accepts you? The deeper our embrace of ourselves is, the happier we are, and the more likely we will parent from a place of honest centeredness and sincerity. The more we are looking for someone else to give us their approval, the less centered, more edgy, and imbalanced we can become.

Thich Nhat Hanh suggests, "to be beautiful means to be yourself. You don't need to be accepted by others." That means giving yourself space to be human and to feel all your emotions, without needing to shape it so that others accept or approve of you. It means that sometimes your house is a mess and your hair is a mess and your kids are a mess. It's okay. Loving our lives with less struggle means that we relax into whatever the situation at hand is. Even if it's not exactly the image we had in our mind when we started.

It's important to note that accepting a situation doesn't mean that you are stuck there, or even that you condone what you don't like; it simply means that you are in touch with reality and that you are still in the process of becoming. It means you "take you as you are," and you train your children to embrace the wholeness of who they are as well. By accepting ourselves and our children "as we are", we free up tremendous energy that can be used to help this world at large, and the microcosm that is your world under your own roof. What a refreshing sanctuary to feel accepted in your own heart, and to offer that embrace to your family. It doesn't mean that there won't be issues to contend with, or that it'll always be a love-fest; but it does mean that when difficulties inevitably emerge, they will do so in the context of acceptance. Think: less anger, less fear, less disapproval. Why not be unapologetic and tenacious in your acceptance of yourself and your family, exactly as you all are in this moment?

Once Cinderella reveals her true identity to the Prince, the narrator says: "The greatest risk any of us can take: to be seen for who we truly are." Seen for who we truly are. In this carefully-crafted culture of Pinterest, Facebook, and Instagram, it's natural to wish to portray an image of perfection for the world to feast on. Problem is that putting on the fake mask separates us from one another and perpetuates the illusion that we are not connected. By revealing who we are in an honest and humble way, we then meaningfully connect to other moms and in fact, all other humans. Much better than photoshopping.

Truth be told, we are at the stage in our lives when it doesn't serve anyone if we hide our true selves from this crazy world. Some might not like our authentic self, but if that is the case, we will find others who do. Not being concerned with the way we are being seen lets us redirect our energy— perhaps in ways to better articulate what is in our heart. I guess you could say, by revealing our true selves, our true tribe will find us.

How do we know when we are not working from our authentic self? I've noticed that the pitch of my own voice is a good "tell." When I'm not operating from a centered "me" space, my voice gets higher and sometimes takes on a nasal quality. But when I'm grounded in my true self, my voice typically takes on a more resonate quality, it's a little deeper and richer. Have you ever noticed how you sound when you're trying to please someone else? It's great feedback from which to find our center. When I'm off, a very simple technique can bring me back to a more embodied place. As I inhale, I consciously feel my hips (if I'm sitting), or the soles of my feet (if I'm standing); this helps me connect with feeling more grounded and then when I speak, it is from an embodied and relaxed center. When we ground first and get into our bodies, our words carry more energy and power. This, in turn, increases our sense of self-respect, a vital aspect of self-acceptance, and allows us to stay connected to our center as we interact with those around us.

And that Fairy Godmother. She is the bomb. Who couldn't use a Fairy

Godmother every now and again to help put things right? What is striking is that she didn't outsource. She could've easily said, "Let's hit Bloomies and get you that dress! Transportation? No problem, we'll order you the white stretch Uber limo, disco ball and all!". Instead, as noticed by many, including Marianne Williamson, the Fairy Godmother rolled up her sleeves and went to work with the raw materials that were right under her nose—which you may recall involved lizards and mice, a pumpkin, and a torn-up dress. She transformed these basic and somewhat unappealing things into the stuff of magic. Fairy Godmother—the original "repurposer."

Much of the time, however, dissatisfaction with how things are going in our family life leads us to look outside of our immediate environment for the fix. We wish for a different time of year, different leadership in our country, a different home, maybe even different people to share our lives with. We can convince ourselves that the answer lies "elsewhere," new and improved, in someone else's newly-remodeled kitchen. There is the hint that we can't enjoy now because we are waiting to be better tomorrow, or calmer next week, or thinner next month, or wealthier next year. This thinking promotes an internal resistance that distracts us from the charms and challenges of our current lives. And you know what happens in that the gulf that is accepting of our lives and resisting our lives? Anxiety is born. That anxiety is a signal that we are no longer present, but trapped in the fantasy of a future self.

The next time the mind-chatter pops up saying that what you have isn't good enough or not as good as it used to be, use anxiety as if it were a call button to get more centered and to deepen your connection to your family, your children, your spouse. Your joy may already be waiting for you in your very own living room right now. Our task is to open and accept our lives, noticing when the mind-clutter is trying to pull us off the love that is already here.

Working with what already is in our lives requires we slow down, have more patience, and creatively open to receive the present moment. By embracing who we are, who our family is, and finding a deeper acceptance of what arises, we are positioned to live our lives with greater maturity and wisdom. Doing so moves us out of the fairytale story and plants us squarely in the real world. We create our own happy ending with a broader perspective that lets us be genuinely ourselves, accepting the woes as well as the wonderful.

HEALING YOGA POSE: *Kalpani Virabhadrasana.* (Scissor Warrior Pose). Come into a high plank (*Dandasana*), with shoulders stacked above your wrists and balls of feet pressing into the ground. Your abdomen is pulled in and you are pushing into the balls of your hands here as well. Draw in a long inhale and exhale. With your next inhale, pull your right knee towards your right elbow. Extend your right leg underneath you, gently placing the outer part of your right hip on the floor. Keep your right knee slightly bent to begin. Next, gently place your left leg on the floor, left knee pointing towards the ground. Place your hands shoulder width apart, in front of your right leg and a few inches away from your torso. Next, gently turn your left knee so your left knee and foot are facing the side wall to your left. From here extend your right leg as straight as possible, so that your right foot extends towards the left side of the room. Pressing down through your palms, externally rotate both shoulders towards the back of your mat. You may feel this pose in your right-side oblique muscles as well as the outer seam of your right leg. To deepen this pose, draw your right leg more towards the top of your mat. Breathe here for 5-10 breaths. Slowly come back to high plank. Rest in child's pose for several breaths. Then repeat on the left side.

BENEFITS: *Releases tension in the side seam of the front leg (the IT band). The twist component aids in digestion. Strengthens upper arms. Opens inner groins. Can release excess heat in the diaphragm and abdomen. Invigorating pose that frees up your energy.*

BE-KIND-TO-YOUR-MINDSPEAK: I love my life just as it is. In a relaxed way, I am transforming and healing my life. I embrace this moment with grace.

Figure 26: *Kalpani Virabhadrasana* (Scissor Warrior Pose)

THE KINDNESS CREW: LESSONS CINDERELLA TAUGHT ME

THE KINDNESS CREW:
From Worried Thinking To Zen Parenting in a Crisis

What solves life's problems is simply to experience the difficulty that's going on, and then to act out of that. We've cut ourselves off from the problem; with all our thinking, reacting, analyzing, we can't solve it. The blockage of our emotional thought makes the problem unsolvable.

Charlotte Joko Beck

Recently, one of my kids was going through something that freaked me out. I was freaking out because there were elements of potential danger in it. I was also freaking out because her experience was reminiscent of something I went through as a teen and so it triggered the wounds of my personal history (which I thought I had already dealt with). It was the perfect storm of stuff from my past, her present, and my fear of the future trajectory. My worried thinking grabbed the wheel of my emotional world.

I got so into my head that not only was my peace of mind during the day interrupted, but my sleep was screwed up at night. Though my heart was in the right place, my worried thinking raked me over the coals—totally exhausting. I guess I'd put up with the coal-raking if it helped my daughter, but as I've come up empty again and again from the well of worried thinking, I know it wasn't helping anyone in a productive way. Instead, worried thinking acted like a jailer, imprisoning me in my own head and separating me from accessing my full body's wisdom.

It's tempting to let the anxiety take over—"What else might go wrong?" "Who is at fault here?", "This train has no brakes!". And "she'll be leaving home soon and what if this continues *out there*?!". To be honest, I kind of wish that worrying fixed the problem because if it did, we'd be in good shape. But, as you know, it doesn't.

In fact, not only does worried thinking throw us off our center, sometimes it can make the situation even worse. We know from neuroscience that worried thinking activates the limbic system (fight, flight, freeze), which, in turn, cuts off more abstract rational thinking. Pretty funny system we have here. No wonder we feel trapped in our own heads when things are seriously challenging. I believe this phenomenon is what Charlotte Joko Beck's writing so beautifully elucidates in the opening quote, and it's exactly what I've and perhaps you, too, have experienced.

What can help us in the trenches of worried parenting? I reached for teachings based on the Zen tradition. Would it be possible to shift attention away from thinking so much and more towards feeling what my body was experiencing in that moment? It was worth a shot. I breathed in and felt the experience. I didn't ignore or deny what was coming up, and conversely, I didn't exacerbate or amplify it either. Instead, I went under the production-line of worried thoughts (it's like a factory in there some days, complete with conveyer belts), and asked myself, where is my body feeling the anxiety? Not the story of why I was anxious, but where was my body feeling the anxiety.

Moving my attention away from the details of the situation and into the way my body was processing the feelings shifted something at a deep level. I noticed that my heart felt heavy, my throat was somewhat tight with anger, my stomach was clenched with anxiety, and the back of my neck twinged with disappointment. What became crystal clear was that my worried mind was actually trying to protect me from feeling all this muck. If I kept myself tantalized (albeit unpleasantly) in my head, I wouldn't have to sink into the heart of these truly uncomfortable feelings. The conveyer belt of worried thinking kept the depth of these sensations at bay.

I breathed into these heavier spaces in my body, almost like I was trying to get to know the feelings that were trapped in there. Ala Thich Nhat Hahn, I said, "hello my little fear, hello my little anger, hello my little disappointment." I gotta admit, this felt kind of cheesy at first, but I have so much respect for Thich Nhat Hahn's work, that I pushed through the initial "fluff." I started to feel a little letting go. But truth be told, staying with the feelings and not getting sucked into the blame-game or dramatic details was like balancing in four-inch heels on an exercise ball in the middle of the ocean. It's a slippery slope. I had to keep reminding myself to stay with the feeling, but you know what? I felt more grounded. I was kindly and sanely relating to myself in the middle of this storm.

Through this grounding I could see my typical responses to the crisis as plain as day—I either buried my anxieties in overthinking or got out my proverbial brass knuckles to punch the feelings in the nose. The pretty amazing thing is that by neither denying nor amplifying, but instead by sitting with the embodied feelings, I felt more relaxed—kind of like the lights are on and I'm actually home. Relaxed maybe because I was experiencing reality exactly as it was, not the way it "should" be as dictated by my ideal image. And, perhaps I felt more relaxed because by taking care of my emotions in this way, I brought less intensity to my interactions with my daughter.

Letting the Zen tradition into parenting is counterintuitive because it feels like the bottom dropped out. And it has in a way—you aren't doing as much as you are used to doing and you're not in worried thinking either. You instead are more aligned with **being and experiencing**—these, the gateways to true loving presence. I think the real trick is to remind ourselves to do this when the worried thinking ramps up. If we do, it becomes a real game-changer. What if the next time worried thinking stole the show, you used it as a signal to get in touch with how your body is feeling and processing the experiences?

HEALING YOGA POSE: *Dekasana*. (Airplane Pose). Start on the right leg for this balancing pose. Bend into your right knee slightly and extend your left leg long behind you. You can aim for your leg to be at hip-height, but anywhere off the ground is great. Your left toes point down towards the floor, and both frontal hip bones face the floor beneath you. Extend your arms out alongside you in a "V" shape, with your palms facing the floor. Can you create a slight backbend in your upper and middle chest, sort of like an upward dog shape? Breathe 10 full cycles of breath here. Put your left foot down next to your right and stand in Mountain Pose, arms alongside you. Take one full cycle of breath to regroup. Repeat with left leg standing and your right leg extended behind you.

BENEFITS: *Strengthens the leg muscles of the standing leg, including the muscles of the standing foot. Enhances the gluteus muscles of both legs. Opens the chest, increases breathing, relaxes the mind. Releases tension in the chest, all the while improving your balance. The backbend component acts as an anti-depressive yoga posture.*

BE-KIND-TO-YOUR-MIND SPEAK: I feel the emotions in my body and say hello to them with love. I am grounded and at home in my body. I breathe in, and breathe out with peace.

Figure 27: *Dekasana* (Airplane Pose)

CELEBRATE YOU

So, honestly, how often do you take time to honor and celebrate yourself? I can tell you that I personally struggle with doing this—not offering myself nearly as much credit, celebration, respect, as I probably deserve (I have a feeling I'm not alone:)).

This section meets this life challenge head on. I'm not talking about necessarily throwing a big party for yourself (although, sure, why not), but about finding the moments in your daily life to celebrate your own essence. Moments where you don't hold back on revealing who you are. This section asks you to bravely confront yourself when you are hiding your beautiful light from others because you don't want to threaten them, or you don't want the pressure associated with being creative, successful, inspired, and all that. This section asks you to notice what you're saying to yourself that might hold you back, and to work with the discomfort that comes up for all of us when we shine our essence. The world becomes a much brighter place when we have the courage to shine on.

CELEBRATE YOU:
Beware the Rainbow Fish

Our deepest fear is not that we are inadequate. Our deepest fear is that we are powerful beyond measure. It is our light, not our darkness that most frightens us. We ask ourselves, 'Who am I to be brilliant, gorgeous, talented, fabulous?' Actually, who are you not to be? You are a child of God. Your playing small does not serve the world. There is nothing enlightened about shrinking so that other people won't feel insecure around you. We are all meant to shine, as children do. We were born to make manifest the glory of God that is within us. It's not just in some of us; it's in everyone. And as we let our own light shine, we unconsciously give other people permission to do the same. As we are liberated from our own fear, our presence automatically liberates others.

Marianne Williamson

I hate that book, *The Rainbow Fish*. You know, it's the story about the most beautiful fish in the sea, whose unique shiny scales evoke such jealousy from his friends, that they reject him, withhold friendship, and ultimately ostracize him. They finally come around and give Rainbow Fish friendship, but only after the Rainbow Fish removes each of these shiny scales and gives a scale to each of his friends. The Rainbow Fish is no longer so shiny, he doesn't stand out in a crowd, he looks like the rest of the fish, and then, the peer group and elders reward him by accepting and praising him for dimming his light. What the What???!!

I get that The Rainbow Fish story is supposed to be about the joys of sharing and that my perspective will evoke anger for some of you. But, keeping it real, The Rainbow Fish conveys a less positive message to my ears. It says, if you shine too bright, those around you won't be able to contain their jealousy and you'll be rejected, isolated, or worse. You want acceptance and love? Then dull what is most magnificent about you, hide your greatest assets, and for God's sake, don't sparkle so bright. Even if it means, as it does with The Rainbow Fish, mutilating yourself.

Maybe you can relate. I certainly can. For years, I covered up my divine sparkle. I let the fear that others might feel threatened by my shine, the fear that others would try to take away my shine, get to me. I'd go into hiding. I still struggle with this urge at times. I know a lot of you hide your sparkle too. We want to protect that wounded part of ourselves that believes it is too risky to shine. Maybe a parent, or sibling or friend was threatened by your success when you were younger. Or maybe you learned from experiences of physical, emotional or sexual abuse that it was too dangerous to stand out because it increased the likelihood that you'd be hurt. The good news is that our unique spark can never be destroyed, but too often we keep it hidden under layers of emotional batting.

Ironically, covering up our divine sparkle doesn't keep us safe. It doesn't even get us the genuine connection we're after. It says to the universe that we don't trust that we're divinely protected and guided. But the truth is that when we bring all of our brilliant faculties to a situation, when we let our beauty shine—we access even greater intuition, power, and divine guidance. It can be daunting at first to let your shine sparkle, but don't use that fear as a signpost to retreat. Rather, the fear is a sign that you need even more encouragement to shine. It reminds you that you're on your path to reclaiming your wholeness. You may say, but what if there

CELEBRATE YOU: BEWARE THE RAINBOW FISH

is a real concern for safety? Good question. Ask yourself from a centered place, is there a current legitimate fear, or is the fear a recycled protective mechanism from the past? Most of the time, the feeling of fear is actually one that will keep us from our greatest destiny. It's the past trying to grip our present moment and keep us imprisoned in its former embrace. (If it is real, then please address it).

Please never doubt that you have something amazing to share. Don't diminish who you are to satisfy someone else's limiting ideas. We each have a unique shimmer and by expressing yours, you free others to find and shine their sparkle too. You might still enjoy reading The Rainbow Fish, but remember that the subtle undertones are there, suggesting that we dim our light. Maybe you would consider counterbalancing reading The Rainbow Fish with the message that all people have a beautiful divine sparkle, and by celebrating the light in our fellow travelers, we actually make this world an even brighter place. You have the power. The power to make the decision, and then make it again and again and again to not spend one more minute dulling what is your birthright—to sparkle and to shine that beautiful essence of yours.

HEALING YOGA POSE: *Trikonasana.* (Triangle Pose). Start in Warrior II, right foot forward. Your left foot is roughly parallel to the back of the yoga mat, with your left heel slightly pushed back further away from the toes. You can align your front heel with the arch of your left foot, though that is not necessary. Your arms are outstretched alongside you. From the hip joints, extend your torso over your right thigh and reach your right hand to your right shin or to a block on the inside of your foot. Turn your left ribs towards the ceiling and slightly behind you as you extend your left hand towards the ceiling. Aim to keep both sides of your side body as long as possible, sending energy through the crown of your head. Push the outer edge of your left foot down into the mat. Now, your thigh and glute muscles. You can look up at your top had, the side wall, or even down towards your right foot. Can you breathe deeply here while lengthening your tailbone towards your left heel? Stay here for 5-8 breaths. Recommit to an engaged core and engaged thighs. To come out of the pose, press down through your back foot, bend into your right knee slightly and rise to standing. Turn and face the back of the room so that your left leg is forward, and your right leg is in the back. Repeat with the left leg forward.

BENEFITS: *Stretches your gluteus medius, the tops of the hip as well as the* *external rotators of the hips. Lengthens the inner groins while strengthening your ankles. Releases stuck tension along the sides of the body, including the neck. Alleviates stress in the back as well as stress in the mind. Increases your confidence.*

BE-KIND-TO-YOUR-MINDSPEAK: Today I give myself the freedom to let my divine sparkle shine bright. With enthusiasm and faith, I shine my true nature to myself and to the world.

Figure 28: *Trikonasana* (Triangle Pose)

CELEBRATE YOU:
Choose Joy

It is important to become aware that at every moment of our life we have the opportunity to choose joy. It is in the choice that our true freedom lies, and that freedom is, in the final analysis, the freedom to love.

Henri J.M. Nouwen

"The house is so quiet now. I have more time than I know what to do with." He looked towards his feet as he continued, "Enjoy them while you have them."

Typically, when I hear this type of suggestion, the cynic in me dismisses it with some snide comment like, "this person has absolutely no clue about raising kids." Yet, this time, something deep within my soul sat up and listened. I chose to let my neighbor's words wash over me with their poignancy, their sadness, their love. A stream of light beamed through a small crack in a room that I hadn't even realized was dark.

A Ghost of My Future Self, my neighbor's words hung heavy in my kitchen. Raise them? Check. Manage their lives? Check. Enjoy them? Er…I heard myself defending myself, well, I'm so busy keeping everything moving and everyone happy! There is so much to do! I don't really have the time or energy to *enjoy* them. Pffff…who has the time to ENJOY them?!!

Of course, no one *wants* their children's youth to be a blurred memory, but sadly because there is less and less time to relax, less time for "leisure", less time to explore who they are and our connection to them, it's increasingly more difficult to enjoy them. Some days my friends and I joke that we feel like a mix between an Uber driver and a drill sergeant. We do our best to see that our kids are eating the right foods, getting enough sleep, not getting too much screen time, hanging with positive people, doing their homework, practicing their saxophone, getting from point A to B (and often to points C, D, and E). That leaves little room to simply stop and be "in joy" with them. Yet, I can't deny the nagging truth that if we're not paying attention, we're going to miss the pleasure in these special years.

We need a radical shift. Like Tracy Chapman, I'm talking about a revolution. No need for signs, or marches—this revolution is in your kitchen, your car, your backyard. It's a two-pronged revolution. It begins with the courage to notice.

The first thing to notice is if we are literally taking on too much. That is, physically too many responsibilities. One surefire way to interrupt your joy is to be overburdened by responsibility. The signal that you are is you'll feel consistently depleted or resentful. We all get here from time to time, but if it's more than every now and again, then it's time to explore another way. Another way might be delegating some of your activities or asking for more instrumental support. Another way might also include honing your capacity to say "Nope, can't help out." Saying no is like a muscle and the more you use it, the more familiar you become with its movement and the more you feel comfortable using it. I truly believe that there is just no way we were put on this planet to run ourselves ragged toward some non-existent finish line. How could we possibly enjoy anything if we have to do *everything*?

Beyond what you're actually doing, the second prong is to notice how you are doing what you are doing. That is the attitude you bring to your tasks. Like many of you, I often had a less-than-positive attitude when taking on some of the more mundane tasks in life. I have friends who love it, but housework and I are not the best buds. Thing is, the negative attitude I have towards laundry and mopping can get lodged in my body as well as unintentionally infuse that activity with my frustration. Like the scene in *Like Water For Chocolate*, when the food gets infused with the energy of the person cooking it—of course, that was a more dramatic representation of this concept, but the insight of infusing our actions with our energy rings true. As Thich Nhat Hanh reminds us, by noticing our thoughts in a mindful way, we can transform them. The slippery slope is to notice without putting yourself down for feeling negatively.

In some cases though, simple awareness of our thoughts just doesn't cut it. We need more. In those instances, set an intention before undertaking any activity. For example, before making dinner, set an intention to find the joy and delight in the fact that you have fresh food, a working kitchen, and children to feed. The mind loves images—so picture yourself happy, finding pleasure in your daily task. Picture your children enjoying the meal you prepared (this is a stretch for me on many nights, as I am living with some seriously picky eaters). You might be thinking, oh it's easy to picture it, but you know it won't work out that way. I get it. The thing is—picturing the attitude you want to have, seeing yourself feeling comfortable and happily engaged, acts like a magnet. And when things don't turn out, it'll be easier to bounce back emotionally and energetically.

Treat it like a Where's Waldo exercise, but instead of looking for a guy in a striped-hat, you're looking for those places where your delight quietly resides. So, when you notice the joy or delight, stop and feel it. For me, I know I've found it when I feel a warmth in the center of my chest, a broad band of something buoyant. I could be doing the most simple of activities, but if my orientation is to be open to the joy, I'll feel it when I wash my hands with warm water and that Verbena soap I love. At other times, it's that joy that comes from hearing my children call me their Mom. Thing is, the more we look for joy, the more we'll find it. Setting an intention can activate the part of the brain called the Reticular Activating System (RAS), which helps us identify certain patterns in our environment. When you set an intention to look for the joy in the simple, even the monotonous, you're essentially giving this part of your brain the command to help you scan your environment for such information and bring it to your attention.

By the way, positioning ourselves to locate joy doesn't mean engaging in denial. Be aware of how you feel. Don't stop there, though. The greatest contemplative thinkers remind us that our joy isn't dependent on the outside circumstances. It is a choice. Choosing the quality of our thoughts—whether they are promoting negative spirals or cultivating uplifting energy makes a huge difference in terms of whether we can enjoy our moments with our children. The kids might not be in a good mood, but that doesn't mean you have to give up your good mood right along with them. They might forget to clean their rooms, but that doesn't mean you can't communicate your wish for orderliness from a centered place, rather than from an angry one (however understandable it is that you might be irritated that you're still saying the same thing 1000 times a week).

Keeping it real, when I started doing this, I was definitely met with a little push back from some of the kids. I explained that I was working on my own happiness and that a happy mom is a better mom. So, if you get a little shove back, it's a good sign. Your efforts are not going unnoticed.

Don't put too much weight on their push back; stay your course and continue to cultivate joy in the moment of their resistance to change. You're modeling something extremely valuable for them and something they actually crave—your happiness.

Our precious life moves fast. By seeking joy in the everyday, we celebrate the simplicity of being alive, of being human. We honor the mundane because, when you think about it, the majority of our lives are spent knee-deep in the simple and the mundane. Rather than letting the ordinary moments get all hazy, use this approach. It will help you bring miracles to the everyday, keep your present, and position yourself to genuinely say, "Thanks, I actually do enjoy my kids and am pumped that I get to be here for them now."

HEALING YOGA POSE: *Ardha Chandrasana.* (Half-Moon Pose). Stand in Warrior II with right foot forward. Place a block 6-12 inches in front of right pinky toe. Place your right hand on the block and lift your left leg up behind. Stack your hips, one on top of the other. Aim to get your left leg parallel to the floor and level to your hip. Reach your left hand to the ceiling. Make sure your right toes are pointing forward to avoid twisting in the standing kneecap. Shoulders are stacked as well. Balancing on your right leg, breathe for 5-7 breaths. Come out of the pose and repeat with your left foot forward.

BENEFITS: *Improves balance. Strengthens butt, leg, thighs of standing leg and opens the hip flexor and groins of extended leg. Creates more buoyancy in the arches of the feet. Opens the front of the chest and expands the capacity to breathe.*

BE-KIND-TO-YOUR-MINDSPEAK: Today, I delight in the simple pleasures of life. I find sweetness in my daily routine and notice small moments of joy and love everywhere.

Figure 29: *Ardha Chandrasana* (Half-Moon Pose)

CELEBRATE YOU:
Shine On You Crazy Diamond

Shine your light as brightly as you can, to be a beacon of hope and inspiration for others.

Doreen Virtue

Did you ever notice how many times you hold back your enthusiasm, your brilliance, your energy, your beauty, your sensuality? Someone offers you a compliment, and you put yourself down, rather than graciously accept. Holding back on pursuing a dream that you've had for decades because you trick yourself into believing some self-imposed limitation about yourself, rather than going for it. Sometimes we even downgrade our children's talents in front of others, because we don't want to provoke them into feeling threatened or competitive.

I see it all the time, and I have done it to myself. I have put myself down for a variety of reasons, often because I didn't want to seem full-of-myself, or because I didn't want to make others feel intimidated. Like many of you may have been, I was seduced by the belief that if I didn't shine, others would be more comfortable around me. I guess you could call it a pre-emptive strike of sorts—I'd take myself down before anyone else had the chance to do it. By my participating in the dance this way, others won't have to worry about stepping up either; they can stay in their space of limiting themselves.

And if we don't threaten others with our amazingness, then we don't have to worry that they will try to outshine us, thereby asking us to step up another notch and perhaps out of our own comfort zone. This is often an overlooked mechanism, but that doesn't make it any less true. In an effort to regain psychological "safety", we sometimes stifle our own flow.

It is easy to say, shine on and don't hide who you are. But until we reveal the hidden costs of shining, we will hold ourselves back. For me, the hidden costs of shining are not just that another will feel threatened—it's that it evokes a feeling that I have nothing unique to add. The fear, in this case, is that my voice can be easily copied, replicated, and perhaps even outdone.

As Maya Angelou so aptly stated, "I have written 11 books but each time I think, 'Uh-oh, they're going to find out now. I've run a game on everybody, and they're going to find me out.'" If you've been there, you know that this thinking creates a gnawing frustration in our lives, and one that may infuse our family life with a sense of agitation. Wouldn't it make most sense to recognize that fear is an integral part of moving out of our comfort zone, and to shine bright anyway? Not only will it show our children that shining bright is the way to make a contribution to this world, but it will also relieve us of the regret that we had something to share but we let fear of failure/success/being found out hold ourselves back.

Let yourself shine today and let that shine illuminate tomorrow and the days ahead. When you see your neighbor or loved one shining, celebrate it as another example of the beauty of God's love for each and every one of us. We are all interconnected. And, we were each born to not hide our light under that blanket, but to find the courage to reveal our light with no apologies, and in fact, with great passion.

HEALING YOGA POSE: *Vasisthasana* (Side Plank Pose). Start this pose in the Downward Dog Pose. On an exhale, lower yourself to plank position, elbows straight and your body in one long line. Now, move onto the outside edge of your left foot, shifting your feet so that your right foot is stacked on top of your left foot. As you do this, turn your upper body so that you are now being supported by your left hand and arm, as well as the side of your left foot. Engage your core and raise your raise your right arm to the ceiling, right hand above your right shoulder, and right palm facing the wall. Pull your shoulder blades towards the front of your chest and slightly downward towards your hips. If this is too much on your wrists, you can build this pose from your forearm. If you're newer to this pose, you can push your feet into the wall for additional support. In any variation, breathe into the pose for at least 10 breaths. Come back into plank and then child's pose. After a few resting breaths, return to Downward Dog Pose and repeat on the other side.

BENEFITS: *Enhances your balance as well as increases your sense of vitality and energy. Strengthens your core, your arms, and your legs. Stretches your wrists as well as your lateral chest muscles.*

BE-KIND-TO-YOUR-MINDSPEAK: We are each unique bearers of light. I am doing my part by shining my best to this world. My brilliance benefits the world.

Figure 30: *Vasisthasana* (Side Plank Pose)

CELEBRATE YOU: SHINE ON YOU CRAZY DIAMOND

NEXT STEPS: In the Letting Go

I realize that there is something incredibly honest about trees in winter, how they're experts at letting things go.

Jeffrey McDaniel

The tiger-striped towel hung sadly in the bathroom towel ring, its silver lines half bleached and side seams bedraggled. I looked at this once cotton masterpiece, this towel I loved—and came to the realization that it's time to get rid of it. A good soldier, it has served its full tour of duty. It has gathered the wet drops of my hands, my husband's hands, the hands of my children, the hands of many loved ones. It has absorbed and dried, absorbed and dried. It's been through 50,000 spin cycles. It's done its job. And yet I can't let this tattered thing go. Not now.

Why can't I trash it? After all, I'm on a tidying-up-clean-out mission and have already let go of things of far more material value. But, this towel. Perhaps it's because I bought this towel when my children were very young and some of my dreams as a younger mom are somehow woven into its fabric. Perhaps it's because letting go of the small inconsequential things reminds us that, whether we like it or not, we must eventually let go of the meaningful and substantial parts of our lives. No one likes to face that reality. Yet, denying it won't make it any less real.

So we breath deeply. Truth is, this life and all its forms are fleeting and impermanent. In fact, everyone and everything in our lives changes, down to the family dog. Our babies are no longer babies; our toddlers are no longer toddlers; even our children in middle childhood give way to adolescence. And those teenagers will fly the coop right before our very eyes. I hate admitting this to myself because I find it painful, but every day is one day step closer to being in an empty nest.

This is very difficult to accept, especially as many of us broadened our definition of ourselves when we became mothers. We took hold of and ran with those roles of nurturer, or provider, of healer, of counselor, as well as those of taxi driver, chef, personal shopper, tutor, and banker, among other things. We know that once they leave the house and get a new address, our lives will be changed forever. Changed in a way that we recognize is a good sign, but is emotionally wrenching, nonetheless. Thing is, despite the hard times, we've loved being the mom of these precious people. They've filled our homes and our hearts with so much laughter, joy, beauty and purpose. Especially purpose. Knowing this is the way the cookie crumbles, it would make the most sense to enjoy each moment as best we can with them now. Exactly how do we relax into the moment so that we can be present for them and for ourselves, so that there are no regrets when the time comes? That is the point of this entry.

From a spiritual and psychological perspective, letting go is healthy, necessary even. Simrad, one of the greatest psychologists of the 1900's, proposed that the inability to let go, to grieve really, prevents us from living our lives now. Perhaps it's the fear that we can't bear the loss, so we dull the connection to the present so that it won't sting so much. That means that part of our mind thinks it's protecting us by encouraging us to turn away from embracing the good that is here. But, based on his science, learning to let go and trusting that we can survive letting go, are the prerequisites necessary if we want to be fully engaged in the now.

I find it most helpful to consider that "letting go" is a skill, and just like any other skill, it can be cultivated with deliberate practice. We practice letting go every time we drop into the present moment, feeling our own internal experience of being in our bodies, and noticing the environment around us.

For a real-time example, think about the letting go of someone or something right now. What comes up for you as you begin to release the grip? For a lot of us, sadness or anger shows up. Let the emotions move through your body. Notice where you feel tension or constriction in your body as you do this exercise. Coach yourself to relax and open. Don't hold onto the feelings, just let them in and let them flow. By relaxing the stop-valve that resists the difficult feelings, we teach ourselves how to keep our hearts receptive. This strengthens the muscle of letting go.

The tiger-striped towel may not hang in the bathroom any longer. But the knowledge that it once was a part of my daily routine, that I felt happy when I saw it, will remain. Our children, as they grow, will not be the little ones that they once were. Both they and we are changed forever by the experience that we shared in this mother-child bond. But by being present to them now as much as possible, we will have less regrets and more memorable moments. We will be full and comforted by memories of how, as younger women, we nurtured and nourished these amazing children. And this will position us to enjoy them even more as they strengthen, test, and enjoy their own wings.

HEALING YOGA POSE: *Ananda Balasana.* (Happy Baby Pose). Lie onto your back, pull your knees into your chest and wrap your arms around them. Roll side to side gently, allowing your lower back and sacrum to make contact with the floor. Inhale and let your knees move away from each other and up towards your armpits. As you exhale, take hold of the outside of each foot with each corresponding hand and allow your knees to open more. Let each ankle move directly above each knee so that your feet are facing the ceiling and your calves are perpendicular to the floor. Flex your feet and push your feet into your hands, at the same time you're pushing your hands into your feet. Relax your lower back into the mat and breathe for at least eight breaths. Can you feel how the earth supports you in the pose?

BENEFITS: *Relaxes the spine into a neutral position while bringing awareness and openness to the inner groins, the hip flexors, and the external rotators. Restores and rejuvenates the spinal column. Deeply soothing and clarifying.*

BE-KIND-TO-YOUR-MINDSPEAK: Today, I cherish my life and trust that the source of all that is good is eternal. I let go of this moment and step into the next one with grace, wisdom and love. I am present.

Figure 31: *Ananda Balasana* (Happy Baby Pose)

ACKNOWLEDGMENTS

When your heart is brimming with gratitude and you know that mentioning a few names just won't cut it. I'm incredibly grateful that I have so many beautiful lights in my life, so many who have inspired me, so many who have helped me find the courage and the steadfastness to birth this paper baby to life. Thank you Mom and Dad (in Heaven), for showing me that love, love, and more love is the answer to many of life's thorny problems. To all my students at the Windsor Club, your dedication and commitment to bringing your true selves to the practice inspires me every time. Thank you to all my friends—especially Julie Plaut-Mahoney, Mia Wenjen, Patricia Howard, Donna Marsh, Christine Fordyce, and the BAEs moms—a sincere depth of gratitude for your encouragement, your honesty, and for consistently believing in me. Huge thanks to Maria Sullivan, who with kindness, courage, and love, has been such an amazing friend and sister to me. Thank you, dear Lena Goodwin, whose editing skills are truly one-of-a-kind exceptional and I'm more than grateful to know you. And a deep well of gratitude to my family—Tim for your phenomenal support and love—through this and every endeavor we undertake in our incredible journey, side by side. Thank you to Julia, Grace and Charlotte, for inspiring me every day to breathe deeply as we learn together on this path towards greater wisdom, love and kindness. I love you all.